Enno Hinrichs

To Rosalind

Preface

✦ ✦ ✦

The sermons in this volume were prepared for radio. They have been selected from those delivered over the Protestant Hour Network in the winter and spring of 1955, and over the National Radio Pulpit in the summer of the same year. Only such editing has been done as was necessary to make them suitable for publication. Consequently, like all sermons, they are intended to be "read with the ear" rather than with the eye. They are offered here at the prompting of some who were kind enough to suggest that these radio addresses would find a reading audience if they appeared in book form.

EDMUND A. STEIMLE

Nantucket, Massachusetts
July, 1956

Contents

+ + +

PART I

+ + +

"My thoughts are not your thoughts . . ."

Naaman, commander of the army of the king of Syria, was a great man with his master and in high favor, because by him the Lord had given victory to Syria. He was a mighty man of valor, but he was a leper. Now the Syrians on one of their raids had carried off a little maid from the land of Israel, and she waited on Naaman's wife. She said to her mistress, "Would that my lord were with the prophet who is in Samaria! He would cure him of his leprosy." So Naaman went in and told his lord, "Thus and so spoke the maiden from the land of Israel." And the king of Syria said, "Go now, and I will send a letter to the king of Israel."

So he went, taking with him ten talents of silver, six thousand shekels of gold, and ten festal garments. And he brought the letter to the king of Israel, which read, "When this letter reaches you, know that I have sent to you Naaman my servant, that you may cure him of his leprosy." And when the king of Israel read the letter, he rent his clothes and said, "Am I God, to kill and to make alive, that this man sends word to me to cure a man of his leprosy? Only consider, and see how he is seeking a quarrel with me."

But when Elisha the man of God heard that the king of Israel had rent his clothes, he sent to the king, saying, "Why have you rent your clothes? Let him come now to me, that he may know that there is a prophet in Israel." So Naaman came with his horses and chariots, and halted at the door of Elisha's house. And Elisha sent a messenger to him, saying, "Go and wash in the Jordan seven times, and your flesh shall be restored, and you shall be clean." But Naaman was angry, and went away, saying, "Behold, I thought that he would surely come out to me, and stand, and call on the name of the Lord his God, and wave his hand over the place, and cure the leper. Are not Abana and Pharpar, the rivers of Damascus, better than all the waters of Israel? Could not I wash in them, and be clean?" So he turned and went away in a rage. But his servants came near and said to him, "My father, if the prophet had commanded you to do some great thing, would you not have done it? How much rather, then, when he says to you, 'Wash, and be clean?'" So he went down and dipped himself seven times in the Jordan, according to the word of the man of God; and his flesh was restored like the flesh of a little child, and he was clean.

II Kings 5:1-14 (RSV)

1.

+ + +

Are You Looking for God?

There is a considerable difference between looking for God and finding him. The widespread interest in religion of all sorts and kinds in America these days is evidence that people are looking for God. But whether people actually find God is another matter. Indeed, it's a question whether you can ever find God until he finds you first!

That is why I'd like to turn to a vivid story all but buried back in the second book of Kings—the story of Naaman and Elisha. It is the story of a man who went looking for God and how God found him instead.

Naaman, we are told, was a "commander of the army of the king of Syria . . . a great man with his master and in high favor . . . a mighty man of valor, but he was a leper." Well, that just about sums up our situation, too, doesn't it? We who in our generation are mighty men of science, business, and technology, are also "mighty men of valor, but . . ."—there's always the "but"!

But—some incurable disease of the soul keeps eating away at us (its outward symptoms as ugly as those of leprosy) which shows up in our apparent inability to control home

3

and family life, or teen-age children, or nations, or atomic energy, to say nothing of ourselves with our inward rebellion and the homesickness which haunts our days.

And so, like Naaman, we turn to religion. For Naaman it was a little captive servant girl who suggested to Naaman's wife, who in turn suggested to her husband, that there was a prophet in Israel who could cure the leprosy. Whereupon Naaman took the steps which seemed obvious to him at the time. He decided that if this God were to be found he ought to be approached in a manner worthy of God—and Naaman! So he proceeded to find God by going round about by way of kings and protocol. He approached the king of Syria who in turn wrote a letter to the king of Israel. Armed with royal protocol and fabulous gifts, "ten talents of silver, six thousand shekels of gold, and ten festal garments," Naaman set out. He figured an audience with the king and some $80,000 worth of gifts was impressive enough for a man of his position and would not fail to impress this Hebrew prophet and his God.

On the face of it, it sounds ridiculous to us, of course. And yet, in our expression of religion, we are always tempted to behave in a manner we think befits God's station and ours. We, too, are tempted to think that our approach to God must be "impressive," particularly if we are even a little impressed with ourselves, and we use everything from liturgies overloaded with pomp and circumstance to ecclesiastical embroidery and hocus pocus to gain this end. And I'm not forgetting the temptations that lie in wait for the clergy, either, with our fondness for the prestige which is supposed to go with the office and the "pulpit tone" which always lurks around the minister's larynx. I suppose

4

the average layman does not appreciate how difficult it is for a minister not to sound like one! The problem arises, however, when we *want* to sound like one. The clergy and laymen alike lend an air of importance to this business of approaching God in a manner which befits God—and us!

So we need not be too surprised by Naaman's temper tantrum when Elisha did not come out and appear before Naaman to "stand and call on the name of his God and wave his hand over the place and cure the leprosy." Naaman was irked because Elisha did not put on an impressive show in connection with the cure. God, he figured, ought to act impressively too! And if we are quite honest with ourselves, we come to expect the same divine flourish on Sunday mornings with our fondness for "impressive" services with their vestments, candles, music, ushers, carnations, and choir.

Please don't misunderstand me. I am a member of a church whose worship is quite formal and I, personally, feel more at home in the liturgical forms which have been handed down to us through the centuries. Moreover, I am aware of the necessity of treading softly here because there is a thin and ambiguous line which divides dignity appropriate to the worship of the high and holy One, and an "impressive" service designed to impress God, ourselves, and any of the neighbors who may drop in. I am only suggesting that it is wise, occasionally, to take a good, long look at our worship to see what we are doing and why.

It may be amusing, for instance, to recall that there is a fifteenth-century sermon which "rebukes certain German nobles because they stood at the epistle to honor St. Paul as being one of their own class!" [1] But what of the over-loaded entrances and exits to our service? Analyzed, they may turn out to be almost as amusing. It takes us such an unconscionable time to get started. When you add up the organ prelude, the silent prayer, the lighting of the candles, a prayer intoned in the entry and its response, a proces-sional hymn, and an invocation and its response, you begin to wonder who's invoking whom! And we seem to have equal difficulty getting out—with the benediction and its response, a recessional hymn, a closing prayer and its response, followed by organ chimes, silent prayer, the dous-ing of the candles, and at length the organ postlude. It's like the preacher who can't get rid of his sermon when he's way past the end of it. Smile as we may at Naaman's tantrum when Elisha failed to provide a divine flourish and impressive ceremony along with the cure, we had best look to ourselves and the way in which we expect to find God before we smile too broadly.

Of course the result of all this is that God almost gets lost. Naaman almost lost him a couple of times. First his approach through kings backfired when the king of Israel suspected some international intrigue was afoot and lost his temper. Then Naaman lost *his* temper because Elisha failed to be impressed by Naaman, his horses, chariots, and fabulous gifts. Elisha did not even come out of the house to greet him, but sent a messenger telling Naaman simply to wash seven times in the revoltingly muddy waters of the Jordan. At that point Naaman was ready to give up and go home.

[1] William P. Ladd, *Prayer Book Interleaves* (New York: Oxford University Press, 1943), p. 145.

Many a lost and lonely soul today wanders into our churches and wanders out again, ready to give up and go home because of our preoccupation with ecclesiastical protocol. The more impressive our services, the more forbidding and cold they're apt to seem to the hungry soul who wanders in hoping to find God. And our preoccupation with kings all too often leaves the plain or even shabby stranger with something less than a warm welcome.

But God didn't get lost for Naaman, because God took a hand in the proceedings. While Naaman was absorbed with kings and protocol, God was working as he always works through the most unlikely people, using the most unlikely methods.

First there was that little, captive, Hebrew servant girl, who whispered to Naaman's wife, who in turn whispered to Naaman, who thought there might be something to the girl's story about Elisha and his God. Naaman covered his embarrassment when he went to the king with this boudoir gossip by trying to pass it off casually: "Thus and so spoke the maid." But Naaman, the mighty man of valor, found the way to God through the unlikely lips of his wife's chambermaid.

Later, when Elisha failed to perform up to his expectations and Naaman flew into a tantrum, it was Naaman's servants who dared to tackle the angry man of valor and whose indisputable logic cleared the air. "If Elisha had asked you to do some great thing?" they asked. "Of course," replied the mighty man of valor. "Then," they suggested, "why not try the ridiculously easy thing and wash in the muddy Jordan as he tells you?" So Naaman

7

washed and found that, for all his looking, God had actually found him through the unlikely lips of his servants.

The story reflects with unerring accuracy God's way with us. While we are preoccupied with kings and protocol, looking for God in impressive places and imposing people, God works in his own way through the most unlikely people. There was Moses, a murderer on the run tending sheep for his father-in-law, reduced to living on his wife's family. Yet God used Moses to stand before Egypt's fabulous Pharaoh demanding that his people be set free. There was Amos, rough and tough, desert-born and -bred, mincing no words with the genteel churchwomen of Samaria, calling them, "you cows of Bashan!" There was Jesus—of Nazareth in Galilee, of all places!—the Son of God and Lord of Lords! And afterwards the thin, red line of martyrs, nameless nobodies, most of them, through whom God spoke and worked while kings and empires, statesmen and generals had their day and ceased to be.

And today God speaks to you often enough where you least expect to hear his voice: through the unlikely lips of your children, perhaps, or in the cries of children playing on the streets in the slums, or on the lips of those twenty-five disfigured girls from Hiroshima. God speaks to you more clearly through these, perhaps, than on the lips of priests and clergy.

Ask a minister sometime how God speaks to him and he'll tell you one instance after another how God speaks to him on the lips and through the lives of ordinary people like yourself. There's a woman, widowed, doing a grand job of bringing up her two young boys, telling me how lonely it is and how God helps. Or there is that little eight-year-old girl, legs paralyzed from polio, dragging herself along on crutches behind the junior choir to sing, "Now thank we all our God."

Or there is that neighborhood tailor I once knew. One day, shortly after the end of World War II, I was in his shop and he stopped me as I was leaving and said in his thick accent, "Mr. Steimle, I have a problem. As you know, I am a Jew and my wife, she is a Christian. Her brother was a violent Nazi. When we were in Germany he hated me and did nothing to help us. He was glad to get rid of us when we came over here. But now he is in a prison camp and he has written us asking us to send him some food. My wife, she says no. We send him nothing. But I say yes. We should send him something. What do you think, Mr. Steimle?" I don't know how you would have felt. I felt humble and ashamed. Ashamed for his Christian wife, of course, but more ashamed of myself that I had not been prepared to hear the voice of God on the lips of a pleasant neighborhood tailor.

God speaks to us through the least likely people and he uses the most unlikely methods. For Naaman, no spectaculars worthy of the divine, just the muddy Jordan. And for us today, no visions, in all probability, with the label "divine" plastered all over them, just ordinary things like . . .

The Bible. The preacher mentions reading the Bible and the reaction is likely to be almost as violent as Naaman's tantrum—in reverse! The yawns, the wandering mind, the utter boredom which come to the faces of the people when the preacher suggests reading the Bible. And yet the Bible with its worn and familiar pages is pregnant, like the muddy Jordan, with health and life if, like Naaman, we can be prodded into plunging into it. Even in some of its least likely sections, the fifth chapter of Second Kings, for instance, it still speaks eloquently to our day.

The Bible—and the sacraments. We tend to think of the sacraments as exotic and extraordinary. And yet we miss the point of them if we do not recognize that the extraordinary thing about them is that God uses the most ordinary of material things—water, bread, wine—to indicate that he always comes to us in the ordinary stuff of life. We live surrounded by the common, material things of life which are the gift of his hands, and these constant reminders of his presence indicate that the spiritual and the material are not two worlds but one.

You see, there is a considerable difference between looking for God and finding him. You and I are always tempted to think God is to be found by way of kings and protocol, that he ought to act the way we would act if we were God, instead of taking him at his word. Naaman found out and so can we. For Naaman, like the prodigal in the far country, came to himself and accepted himself for what he was in the eyes of God, no captain of the host or man of distinction but simply a man in need of health. It's all God asks, you know. Just that you come to him without pretensions or gifts, simply as a soul in need of his health. And he will cleanse you, too.

O the depth of the riches both of the wisdom and knowledge of God! How unsearchable are his judgments, and his ways past finding out! For who hath known the mind of the Lord? Or who hath been his counsellor? Or who hath first given to him, and it shall be recompensed unto him again? For of him, and through him, and to him, are all things: to whom be glory for ever. Amen.

Romans 11:33-36

2.

+ + +

Creeds and God's Mystery

I suppose there is no more unexciting if not downright un-
popular aspect of religion than that of creeds and doctrines
and dogma. To the sensitive and searching soul the very
word "dogma" suggests all kinds of unpleasantnesses from
the closed and intolerant mind to the high and forbidding
barriers erected by hidebound churchmen across the portals
of their churches. And so these thoughts are directed to
the man who instinctively puts up his guard and gets on the
defensive whenever the words "creed" or "dogma" are
used in connection with religion.

To begin with, let's get over the idea that dogma is a
nasty word just because it can be, and often is, misused.
Freedom, for example, has a fine ring in our ears but freedom can be, and often is, misused too. When it is, it also
leads to all kinds of unpleasantnesses from utter anarchy
and chaos in a schoolroom to unruly mobs and ugly lynch-
ing parties.

Moreover, creeds and dogma are part of the common life
of every one of us. There are certain facts about life which
every last one of us holds to be true. That, of course, is

13

what the word "dogma" means. As an American, you believe that all men are created free and equal. That is dogma. You believe that every child has the right to an education. That is dogma. You believe that you have the right to vote for whomever you choose come next November. That is dogma. Moreover you will fight to the death in defense of these dogmas just as Americans have done in years past.

Well, there are certain dogmas or articles of faith which Christians hold to be true, too. This doesn't mean that a man is asked to close his eyes and swallow them without thinking, like a child taking a dose of castor oil. Rather, consider them as certain facts about God which Christians have found to be true in their own experience in centuries past and still find to be true in their own experience today. Suppose we get at it this way. Many of us are in the habit of pulling out road maps to plot a weekend or vacation trip in the car. It is probably a safe guess that almost every weekend literally millions of us will pull a road map out of the glove compartment to find the best way to reach some delightful spot in the mountains, in the country, or by the seashore. You and I use these road maps as a matter of course, scarcely stopping to think that they are bits of colored paper on which are traced, in effect, the experience of hundreds of thousands of other travelers who have journeyed over these roads before us.

Of course you don't have to use them. You can simply start out in the general direction you want to go, following your nose or stopping now and then to ask directions. Whether these directions help you or not depends on whom you ask. If your experience has been anything like mine, you will often wander off into dead-end streets or into back roads ending up in somebody's barnyard, as the result of garbled directions picked up at the roadside. In fact, I have become something of a trial to my wife because, like some other men I know, I have come to trust my own sense of direction rather than take the time to stop and ask for information. Sometimes it works and when it does I become maddeningly smug. But sometimes it doesn't and I get off into dead-end streets and back roads which lead nowhere and then it's my wife's turn to become maddeningly smug. You see, if you want simply to meander through the countryside, that's one thing. But if you want to get some place without getting lost along the way, the best course, usually, is to pull out the road map.

The dogmas or creeds of the church are something very much like these road maps. They plot the experience of thousands of Christians who have traveled life's highway before us and have left these guides for us to use in our quest for a vital experience of God. You don't have to use them. You can follow your nose, trust your own sense of direction, or stop and ask anyone who happens along. But if you really want to find God, it does seem foolish, doesn't it, just because the word "dogma" has an unpleasant sound in your ears, to disregard the experience of thousands upon thousands of others who have found these creeds and dogmas a trustworthy guide to a vital experience of God?

Take for example what Christians call the doctrine of the Trinity. I suppose there is no Christian dogma which sounds to the average person more mechanical and unreal: "God in three persons, blessed Trinity." It sounds like a mathematical formula. It sounds as if there were three

gods in one, or as Paul Scherer once put it, as if the Father
and the Son sat down in conference occasionally and sent
the Holy Spirit off on an errand. And yet if we use the
analogy of the road map, the doctrine of the Trinity simply
attempts to plot the experience of others like you and me
who have had an experience of the reality of God. Let's look
at it for a moment.

Here is this fabulous world of nature about which we
have come to know so very much so very rapidly in the
past few decades. We have been accustomed to look at
it, of course, through the eyes of science as one amazing
discovery has tumbled over another: plastics and radar,
antibiotics and television, nuclear fission, orthopedic surgery,
and all the rest of it. And yet for the Christian, science is
simply reading God's thoughts after him. And each amazing discovery only serves to increase our awe in the
presence of the God who created not only this vast universe
with its fascinating mysteries but also human minds capable
of probing those mysteries. So Christians in ages past and
today, looking up at the stars or at the amazing wonder of
the human mind, have said, "We believe in God, Maker
of heaven and earth."

But this alone does not tell us very much about the kind
of God that he is. For here are the affairs of men and of
nations stretching down the long corridors of time to the
beginnings of human history. We recognize of course the
interplay of economics, population trends, social factors,
geopolitics, and what not, all determining to some degree the
destiny of peoples and civilizations. Yet with every passing
year it becomes increasingly apparent that this whole vast
stream of human history with its ever more destructive wars

and its ever more pathetic memorial days, with its eternal conflict between good and evil, makes little or no sense except on the basis of one man, born in an off corner of the world, who lived a scant thirty-three years almost two thousand years ago—Jesus Christ.

Whenever men are ushered into the presence of Jesus Christ they do one of two things. Either they shrug him aside as an impractical idealist or they get down on their knees. Christians in ages past and today have said that in this man God entered into human history in a way in which he has never done before or since to reveal his very heart to men. In this man who divides the calendar of the Christian world we believe God has acted to disclose that which is at the heart of this vast universe—the love which at once judges men and nations and also saves those who follow him in obedience and trust. Consequently, we say, "We believe in Jesus Christ, his only Son, our Lord."

But this, too, is not all men have experienced of God. For here is this baffling and bewildering present with a life to be lived, your life and mine, and decisions to be made at every turn. And although you and I are tugged this way and that by fears and desires and selfish ambitions there is within us this strange and wonderful Presence, prompting, guiding, strengthening. Although you ignore it or try to run away from it or rebel against it, yet it never deserts you. It pricks and goads you when you are selfish or proud and leads you to acts of love and sacrifice and heroism you never dreamed possible. And this, too, Christians in ages past and today have called God—the same God who created this fabulous world of ours, the same God who disclosed his innermost character on a cross. And so we say, "We believe in the Holy Spirit, who proceedeth from the Father and the Son."

This, then, is the road map Christians down through the ages have charted for us as a clue to their experience of God: Father, Son, and Holy Spirit—yet one and the same God.

Let us go a step further. A road map, valuable as it may be, is no substitute for the experience itself. You can open up a map and sit and dream over it and never get out of your armchair. You can also recite the Apostles' Creed backward and forward in seven languages and not have the foggiest notion of the God the creed is talking about until you get up and make the venture of life on the basis of it.

Nor is a road map any guarantee your experience will be precisely the same as that of the man in the next car who is traveling along the same road. One man will use the map to get to Yosemite and back again as fast as possible without really seeing anything along the way except the speedometer and the route signs. It is like that cartoon I saw of a car traveling rapidly through one of our scenic national parks with one of the occupants remarking to the driver, "If we hurry we can get around the park in one day and then get an early start in the morning." But another man will actually find the same map a guide to spots of breath-taking beauty and grandeur.

These creeds and dogmas are useful only if they serve as a guide whereby you can come to the place where in your own experience you are carried away by the breathtaking beauty and grandeur of God. There is a passage in the New Testament where that is precisely what happens. In his letter to the Romans, Paul is wrestling with the strange and wonderful ways of God. It is a closely reasoned argument and Paul brings a sensitive and well-ordered mind to the task. But then he suddenly breaks off and his heart overflows his mind in a succession of exclamation points: "Oh the depth of the riches both of the wisdom and knowledge of God! How unsearchable are his judgments and his ways past finding out! . . . For of him, and through him, and to him, are all things: to whom be glory for ever. Amen."

You see, these exclamatory sentences were all Paul found left to say about the ways of God after he had struggled with the whys and wherefores of God's wisdom, judgment, and love. Because for all of our knowledge and experience of God as they are expressed in creeds and dogma, he is always beyond us, beyond our understanding and reason, beyond all our neat little blueprints and formulas.

Which brings me to this: Never be misled into supposing that we Christians think we have God all neatly packaged and labeled for easy distribution and consumption like a package of frozen peas. Our creeds and dogmas only serve to lead us into the "depth of the riches" of God's being. There is a mystery about the nature and ways of God that you and I can never expect to fathom entirely—otherwise God would not be God. We do but touch the fringe of his garment. But we do believe that the fringe which we touch is real!

Harry Emerson Fosdick once described it as being like a man standing on the beach at the edge of the Atlantic Ocean. This little portion of the coast line and the ocean which touches it, I know. This is real. But beyond it are incalculable miles of shore line and ocean which I can never know intimately and about which I can only surmise. These two things I know about the ocean and God: This portion which touches me is real; beyond it is far, far more than I can ever know.

The creeds and dogmas of the church, then, are no pat formulas which provide all the neat answers man can ever find as to the nature of God. Nor are they barriers bearing the legend, "Thus far; no farther." Rather are they invitations to adventure, a kind of spiritual road map offering you the experience of others who have found a rich and exciting experience of God. If you dare the venture, it will lead you, like Paul, beyond bare statements of belief into ecstatic phrases and exclamation points as the only possible result of that venture so that you, too, will exclaim, "Oh the depth of the riches both of the wisdom and knowledge of God! How unsearchable are his judgments and his ways past finding out! For of him, and through him, and to him, are all things: to whom be glory for ever. Amen."

For the kingdom of heaven is like unto a man that is an householder, which went out early in the morning to hire labourers into his vineyard. And when he had agreed with the labourers for a penny a day, he sent them into his vineyard. And he went out about the third hour, and saw others standing idle in the market place, and said unto them: Go ye also into the vineyard, and whatsoever is right I will give you. And they went their way. Again he went out about the sixth and ninth hour, and did likewise. And about the eleventh hour he went out, and found others standing idle, and saith unto them, Why stand ye here all the day idle? They say unto him, Because no man hath hired us. He saith unto them, Go ye also into the vineyard; and whatsoever is right, that shall ye receive. So when even was come, the lord of the vineyard saith unto his steward, Call the labourers, and give them their hire, beginning from the last unto the first. And when they came that were hired about the eleventh hour, they received every man a penny. But when the first came, they supposed that they should have received more; and they likewise received every man a penny. And when they had received it, they murmured against the goodman of the house, saying, These last have wrought but one hour, and thou hast made them equal unto us, which have borne the burden and heat of the day. But he answered one of them, and said, Friend, I do thee no wrong; didst not thou agree with me for a penny? Take that thine is, and go thy way: I will give unto this last, even as unto thee. Is it not lawful for me to do what I will with mine own? Is thine eye evil, because I am good? So the last shall be first, and the first last: for many be called, but few chosen.

Matthew 20:1-16

3.

+ + +

God's Judgments — and Ours

If the Bible has anything at all to say to us, it is to place before us the mind of this mysterious "Other" which we call God. But so much of the Bible has become so familiar that ordinarily it fails to startle us with its "otherness" at all. It speaks of loving our neighbor, of showing mercy to the poor and neglected, of the dire consequences of sin, and of the glories of eternal life. And as it runs along, we run alongside nodding cheerily and often sleepily, "Fine thing, the Bible; says just what it ought to say; says just about what I think about life too." And the mind of this "Other" does not seem strange or alien at all.

Until you come running along and collide with a passage like this parable of the laborers in the vineyard with its haunting refrain, "The last shall be first and the first last." And even the most self-contented mind suddenly realizes that it has had a head-on collision with an entirely different way of looking at things—with God's way of looking at things. God is a father, so Jesus taught. But His ways are not our ways. There is a radical difference for example, between our way of judging people and God's. And it is this problem, the difference between God's judgments and ours, that I want to explore with you now.

You know how we judge people. We stand in the middle of our world and draw a horizontal line across it, normally just about at our eye level. This horizontal line is the standard by which we judge others. Those who come up to the line, we approve. Those who fall below the line, we disapprove. Every day of our lives we go about judging other people on this horizontal basis, approving or disapproving our children's friends, approving or disapproving the actions of our neighbors, approving or disapproving the lives of those who are members of a church. If a man measures up, regardless of his background, he's fine. If he doesn't, he's an undesirable or a bum.

So in our schools. The horizontal line is the passing grade, the diploma at the end of the course. Either a youngster measures up to the horizontal standard or he fails.

So, too, in our courts of law where an effort is made to administer justice as fairly as possible on the basis of the evidence at hand. Here again the horizontal line is drawn. Those above the line are good, upright citizens who pay their taxes and keep out of jail; those below the line are suspect; shady characters, criminals. Granted that some attempts are made in our courts to judge on the basis of motive, and granted that no other system of justice is possible, humanly speaking, than this horizontal basis where a man either measures up or he doesn't measure up on the basis of evidence, God's judgments are still radically different even from the highest standards of justice in our courts.

Now let us take a closer look at this parable where the

basis for God's judgments is made clear. Here is this quixotic character, the master of the vineyard, who goes out early one morning to hire laborers when men are in a position to bargain with him for their wages. And they agree upon half a dollar, let us say. (Labor was cheap in those days!) Later in the morning the master goes out again. This time the laborers are in a less favorable position to bargain and they go off to work merely on the promise of a fair wage. The master of the vineyard repeats this performance at intervals during the day, hiring the last group just before quitting time because there had been no opportunity for them to work earlier in the day.

Then comes the reckoning. The eccentric employer calls those who were hired last to be paid first and gives them exactly what the first had bargained for—half a dollar. The same quaint procedure follows with the rest until those who had been hired first come for their pay and they receive exactly what they had bargained for, half a dollar, the same as those who had worked only a small part of the day. Immediately there is murmuring, something about the injustice of it. But the employer is unmoved. And Jesus concludes it all with, "So the last shall be first and the first last."

The story does not mean that God is a quixotic, eccentric old gentleman giving out rewards according to the whim of the moment. It is, rather, a vivid description of the difference between God's judgments and ours. God's way of judging people is based on tests radically different from ours. The story suggests that whereas our judgments are generally pronounced on a horizontal basis, God's judg-

25

ments are invariably based upon vertical standards, each man by himself without regard to others.

Now what are these standards? First, the parable indicates that God's judgments are based not so much on what a man actually accomplishes as upon his motive. If a man thinks he is in a position to bargain with God, then that which he bargains for he will receive, and no more. But a bargain with God is always a bad bargain. Not that God does not live up to his promises, but the man is never satisfied with his end of it because the man thinks horizontally and compares what he gets with what others get, and it always seems unjust. Whereas if a man simply accepts the assurance of just treatment, that trust will be abundantly justified.

God may know the number of hairs on your head; the flight of a sparrow may not escape his notice. But God, contrary to the ideas some people hold, keeps no ledger with credit and debit columns in which our accomplishments and failures are duly noted. God has far deeper methods for measuring a man than that. Always it is not results, primarily, but the motives behind the results which measure a man's worth in his eyes. God is possessed by the apparently strange notion that once a man's motives are in the clear, the results will take care of themselves.

How many times shall I forgive? Until seven times? "No," Jesus replied, "seventy times seven"—and he didn't mean that we could stop forgiving the four hundred and ninety-first time! Get forgiveness into your very system until it is the controlling motive behind your actions.

Or here is a man who gives $1,000 or $10,000 to a worthy cause: hospital, children's home, church. Measuring this man horizontally, the community calls him a philanthropist because he gives so much more than the rest of us. God might call him a philanthropist, too, or he might call him a miser, depending upon the motive behind his apparent generosity. Or bring it down to our level. You and I are usually keen to know what others in our situation are giving to the local community chest. Why? So we can measure our giving horizontally against the average. It's nonsense! One dollar a month may be a sacrifice for one, and no more than a tip to a hat-check girl for another. Behind the concrete evidence which is seen by others is the unseen motive, and that is what counts in God's eyes. Not, how am I doing in forgiveness or kindness or patience or generosity in comparison with others, horizontally; but in vertical terms, in terms of me, alone, and God. And God, looking down behind the visible evidence into the motives of a man to see what is going on there leads Jesus to conclude: "Many that are first shall be last, and the last, first."

The story also suggests another standard of divine judgment, according to the measure of each man's opportunity. And again the outward evidence may be totally misleading. Some men are born with brains and health; some have the advantage of good family and devoted parents, of financial security and education. Others, however, neither so strong nor so talented, may be crippled by circumstances from the very start; handicapped by a broken home, poor health, a colored skin. Perhaps they would serve God but cannot serve him as they would. "No man hath hired us."

Some of us, for instance, who seem to be such very nice, honest, sincere, kind, clean-living people, may in fact have made so little of our opportunities that we are worse off in

God's eyes than the psychopath who is in prison for attacking a seven-year-old girl. Can it be possible? Remember that Jesus gave more encouragement to a streetwalker than he did to the priest in the temple. "No man hath hired us" —what a world of tragedy is contained in that little sentence. The opportunities which you and I may take for granted as our birthright are denied by heredity or circumstance to others.

It's just that you and I judge a person by the results which a man achieves according to a horizontal standard. Possibly we have to. A man is honest or he is a thief. A man is sincere or he's a hypocrite. A man is dependable or he's unstable. And we hire and fire, recommend or condemn on the basis of it. In our world we have to have some horizontal standards to keep order in our communities. But don't jump to the conclusion that God judges by the same horizontal standard. The point that Jesus is making here is that there will be surprises in store for all of us. For God judges a man vertically, according to a man's motives and according to the measure of his opportunity.

And if you ask me why, I can only answer this: Because God is love. He alone is in a position to judge because he alone completely understands and sees into the very marrow of your character; sees there the opportunities you have had and what you have made of them; sees there the battles you have fought—and won, and the battles you have run away from. He doesn't compare you with anybody else; he loves you too much for that. He simply looks deep into what you really are and knows you even beyond what you know of yourself.

But when you and I stand before the eyes of such a God,

though on the evidence of our lives men may applaud us or condemn us, you and I will know that what God judges us to be is true and righteous altogether.

And getting into a boat he crossed over and came to his own city. And behold they brought to him a paralytic, lying on his bed; and when Jesus saw their faith he said to the paralytic, "Take heart, my son; your sins are forgiven." And behold, some of the scribes said to themselves, "This man is blaspheming." But Jesus, knowing their thoughts, said, "Why do you think evil in your hearts? For which is easier, to say, 'Your sins are forgiven,' or to say, 'Rise and walk'? But that you may know that the Son of man has authority on earth to forgive sins"—he then said to the paralytic—"Rise, take up your bed and go home." And he rose and went home. When the crowds saw it, they were afraid, and they glorified God, who had given such authority to men.

Matthew 9:1-8 (RSV)

4.

+ + +

Arise and Walk

"For which is easier, to say your sins are forgiven; or to say arise and walk?" There's not much question, really, is there? Of course it's easier to say, "Your sins are forgiven," than to say, "Arise and walk," if in the saying more than the sound of words is conveyed and something is supposed to happen. The church declares it every Sunday and in a hundred thousand churches Sunday after Sunday, "Your sins are forgiven." But in how many churches is the paralytic given strength to rise and walk Sunday after Sunday? The question, which is easier, seems to answer itself. But let us take a look at it anyway.

The healing of a paralytic brought to Jesus by his friends throws into dramatic contrast our Lord's attitude to the world's need and our own. Looking at the unfortunate before him, Christ addressed himself first to the hopeless emptiness in the man's eyes, rather than to his obvious physical distress of not being able to walk. "Take heart, my son, your sins are forgiven." Only afterward did he turn his attention to the man's physical distress, "Arise, take up your bed and go home."

31

As in a tiny capsule, this little incident contains the very essence of our Lord's approach to the world's need—to your need and mine. I do not want in any way to minimize our Lord's concern for the material and physical need of mankind. He was abundantly concerned with the plight of human suffering on the level of purely physical suffering. "He took compassion on them" is a commonplace in the Gospels. And yet there can be little question that on the basis of the whole tenor of his ministry, his primary concern was spiritual—and by that I do not mean "otherworldly," divorced from the material and physical needs of mankind. I mean rather that, in his eyes, the two were always linked together, the one the outward expression of the other. And so although it may appear that his primary concern was to save souls and only incidentally bodies, actually his concern was with both. But there was not much point in grafting skin over an ulcer. There was not much to be gained, for example, in healing this man's paralysis if thenceforth he was to walk around on sound legs but with emptiness in his eyes, not knowing where he should walk or why.

Now in contrast, you and I and the rest of us in our world have gone ahead on quite the opposite assumption. We have taken for granted that the basic problem is not the soul's distress but rather the needs of the body. Although it may indeed be easier to say, "Your sins are forgiven," we have applied ourselves with no little success to what is apparently far more difficult, saying to men, "Arise and walk."

And what tremendous strides we have taken here in America in attacking the apparently more difficult part of the question. We have abolished slavery in its crude form of buying and selling human lives. We have also all but done away with economic slavery in the form of child labor, sweatshops, Okies, and sharecroppers. We have dotted the country with hospitals and provided health services for the poor so that the death rate per thousand has dropped some 5 per cent in the past twenty-five years. With every passing year you have more mornings in your lifetime when you will arise and walk than did your father or grandfather.

Or comes a sudden disaster, a flood in Kansas, a hurricane in Rhode Island, and not only does the Red Cross spring into action but all the country's resources are brought to bear to alleviate the suffering. A drunken derelict falls under the wheels of an automobile and we don't wait on the chance that a Good Samaritan may pass by and offer help—an ambulance is on the spot in a matter of minutes to whisk the unfortunate to the hospital to enable him to rise and walk even if only to the corner bar again. The items could go on: housing developments, blood banks, social security, polio, heart, and cancer funds. All testify eloquently to our concern that every man shall be able to rise and walk.

At this material level of our need the picture is bright and getting constantly brighter. We have learned to say with astonishing ease, "Arise and walk." And yet for all that and all that, we find that, in this enlightened and physically comfortable year of our Lord, the eyes of men are frighteningly empty and fearful. The political demagogue with his chosen whipping boy finds a ready-made following to grasp security at the expense of freedom and justice. And those who refuse to go along with the demagogues pull in their horns lest they be associated with the whipping boy.

In one Midwestern university recently, seven organizations for political and social action folded up and three more were on the verge of it—in one year!—for fear that their members might be associated with the whipping boy, the political and social liberal. Moreover, the vacuum in men's souls is currently sucking in all kinds of religious quacks who have never "had it so good." And though our physical health in America is constantly improving, our mental health is showing apparent deterioration. Teen-age delinquency is certainly more than a passing problem.

Add to this the widely accepted practice of income tax evasion among the respectable, stir well, add a pinch of the customary and accepted corruption in civic governments, season with discrimination against minority groups, garnish with the widespread traffic in dope—and you've got as smelly a mess as anyone would care to have put under his nose.

It's a great temptation at this point to pull out all the stops and say that the present situation in this country is the worst ever from the point of view of our spiritual need. Some of us recall, however, the Teapot Dome, the prohibition days of Al Capone, speak-easies and gangland massacres, and some other periods in our history—after the Civil War, for instance, when all was scarcely sweetness and light. One factor, however, may make the situation more serious today. For good or ill, leadership in world affairs has within the past decade been thrust upon us. The plight of freedom in the world rests precariously upon the shoulders of a country which is jittery and unsure of itself, the health of whose character is hardly robust.

Our bodies have never been more comfortable in the

easiest of chairs and the softest of mattresses but our minds are restless and fearful, if not bored, and our spirits are frighteningly empty. We live longer than ever before but we're not so sure any longer for what purpose we live. When a sensitive and intelligent young woman who has been recently married writes and asks in all seriousness whether it is right to bring a child into a world like this, you begin to recognize the depth of the emptiness in the eyes.

We have not been blind to this either, and have provided our own remedies. We have, for example, provided for ourselves a billion-dollar entertainment industry whose prime function is admittedly to provide an escape, an opportunity to forget ourselves and the soul-sickness of our time. Up to a few years ago we had to stir ourselves and go out for this escape, but with typical efficiency we now have brought the entertainment right into our own living rooms so that we can escape everything without moving an inch. Before long, they say, we shall be able to escape in full color and after that, no doubt, in three dimensions too.

Or, perhaps, we are made of sterner stuff and will not allow ourselves to fall so low as to seek mere entertainment as an escape. So we throw ourselves into business or profession, whether housewife, lawyer, businessman, career girl, or laborer, but at the end of the day we are jittery and tense, not merely physically tired, and so have provided the cocktail hour or the couple of beers on the way home from the job as a national institution to provide—what? An appetite? Or possibly an escape from the bleak dulness of a dinner and evening at home dead sober? My intent here is not to condemn the practice but rather to try to analyze the reasons behind it in the light of the gospel.

Or, perhaps, failing to escape, we resort to the psychologist or the psychiatrist who have done wonders for us. But when they bring us to face reality, as they do, and reveal the hidden unpleasantness in our past and tell us to accept it, even though we face it and accept it, it is still there! Who will cleanse it? Or if we are led to see that the basis for our present emotional or mental unrest lay in an overbearing or neurotic parent, who will cleanse their guilt? Or ours—as we repeat the same dreary mistakes in the rearing of our own children?

Which *is* easier to say, "Arise and walk," or to say, "Your sins are forgiven?" And what relevance does the word, sin, have for this soul-sickness which keeps dogging the healthiest, longest-lived, most comfortable, and most efficient society the world has perhaps ever known?

Looking beyond its more obvious expressions, is not sin essentially this: The denial that God means for you to have, precisely where you are and in what you are now doing, an abundant life of joy and significance on his terms, not yours? Is not sin the denial that in the middle of the dishpan, the assembly line, the paper work in the office, the drudgery of preparing for examinations, or in the period of military service—that precisely *there* is the abundant life, the joy our Lord promised to us which, as someone puts it, "worn by the believer like a halo as unfelt as his hair?"

Is not unbelief called the greatest of sins simply because we refuse to believe that this is so? For in our view the abundant life of joy and significance is always someplace else! In California or Florida or Reno; in vacations rather than in midterm; in making a place for ourselves in a career always a rung or two up the ladder rather than in the

36

acceptance of a life of love precisely where we are now at this moment. Is not sin precisely this: The faithlessness that constantly seeks to escape the humdrum monotony of a life that never has within itself at this moment the meaning and significance we think it ought to have.

It is this sin: Your life, my life, disfigured by the denial that it is within itself valuable, significant, and even beautiful in the eyes of God. Your life, my life, disfigured by the tensions set up through discontent and frustration, warped by the drive to carve out for ourselves a place in the sun on our own terms. It is this which is cleansed, set right. You cannot do it, not of yourself. Only God can do it through forgiveness—the easiest, the cheapest (in our ordinary use of the term), yet the most profound word in the Christian vocabulary.

And this is what draws men constantly to the cross, for in its shadow there is a strange peace. Here a man can know that he is accepted. That is what forgiveness, in its simplest terms, means: acceptance. Not because of your brains, your wit, or your good looks, not for the figure you cut on campus or in a career, not because you are "good," certainly, or even because you may be "better" than somebody else, but simply because you are you, irreplaceable, infinitely worth-while in the eyes of God.

The simplest and, I suppose, still the best analogy is the young child who is blessed with wise and loving parents; the child who, regardless of whether he is dull witted or bright, homely or handsome, devilish or well behaved, knows that he is accepted, loved, and constantly forgiven by his parents. And it is that child who, with an assurance he does not consciously recognize, bounds out of the house to play in the sun or hops off to school in the rain, not even aware that the reason why his life has daily joy and purpose and direction is just because he is accepted, forgiven, and loved.

This is the assurance, the "peace of mind," if you like, the cross bestows upon those who linger in its shadow. For here we know it doesn't come easily. It costs. It costs suffering and rejection and death before we will kneel down and accept it, before our defenses come down and we are willing to accept the fact that we are accepted just as we are.

But you are not to remain prostrate at the cross, overcome with remorse and the wonder of it. Acceptance, as with the young child, in itself implies the word of action, "Arise and walk." It means to get up and go about whatever business you may have with new zest, with confidence and purpose and joy—a new creation.

Call it "salvation," call it whatever you like. This is the primary need of our world—your primary need. This is what Christianity has to offer. In a sense, this is *all* Christianity has to offer. The rest of it is commentary.

This is why Jesus addresses himself first to the soul's need, "Take heart, my son, your sins are forgiven," and then sends that cleansed soul out on sound legs, even as he sends you and me back to the same world, the same home, the same job, the same life. But now we go with purpose and meaning in our eyes to face the overwhelming burden and problems of our world with joy in our hearts and a song on our lips—confident that we are no longer a part of the problem but a part of God's creative answer to the needs of our time.

PART II

+ + +

"By the rivers of Babylon . . ."

Then was Jesus led up of the spirit into the wilderness to be tempted of the devil. And when he had fasted forty days and forty nights, he was afterward an hungred. And when the tempter came to him, he said, If thou be the Son of God, command that these stones be made bread. But he answered and said, It is written, Man shall not live by bread alone, but by every word that proceedeth out of the mouth of God. Then the devil taketh him up into the holy city, and setteth him on a pinnacle of the temple, and said unto him, If thou be the Son of God, cast thyself down: for it is written, He shall give his angels charge concerning thee: and in their hands they shall bear thee up, lest at any time thou dash thy foot against a stone. Jesus said unto him, It is written again, Thou shalt not tempt the Lord thy God. Again, the devil taketh him up into an exceeding high mountain, and sheweth him all the kingdoms of the world, and the glory of them; and saith unto him, All these things will I give thee, if thou wilt fall down and worship me. Then Jesus saith unto him, Get thee hence, Satan: for it is written, Thou shalt worship the Lord thy God, and him only shalt thou serve. Then the devil leaveth him, and, behold, angels came and ministered unto him.

Matthew 4:1-11

5.

+ + +

The Peril of Ordinary Days

One of life's commonest experiences is the letdown. After peak days like a graduation, a wedding, or a promotion come the humdrum ordinary days again with the inevitable letdown. Some people seem to have considerable difficulty accepting this fact of human experience. They refuse to adjust themselves to it and consequently live miserable lives while yearning for hours of excitement in which they can take the center of the stage and bask in the glory of it.

Now this same fact of human experience is a part of a man's religious life too. In the life journey of the soul there are luminous moments of inspiration when God seems near and real. But those moments are always followed by a letdown. And if ever you are going to be tempted to lose faith in God, nine times out of ten it will not be in moments of crisis when action or unusual courage is demanded, but rather in periods which the mystics call the "dry periods"— the days when nothing much happens and God seems far away and unreal. That is the peril of ordinary days because it is then that it is the easiest thing in the world to lose faith in God.

That is why the temptation of Jesus in the wilderness speaks so eloquently to our situation. Possibly at no other point in his life did our Lord stand so close to our own experience as here. To be sure, you and I may not be able to understand or appreciate fully the dimensions of the struggle that he went through in those forty days. But in the timing of it and in its dull and dreary setting it speaks directly to the hazards of my own spiritual life and to yours, too, I suspect.

Note, in the first place, that little word, "then." "*Then* was Jesus led up of the Spirit into the wilderness to be tempted. . . ." The temptation in the wilderness followed immediately after a peak day for our Lord—the glory and the exaltation of his baptism. Yesterday it was the heavenly glow and the divine assurance, "This is my beloved Son in whom I am well pleased." Today there is no heavenly glow, no divine voice giving its reassurance. Today it is a lonely man in the wilderness, sure that he hears a different voice: "*If* thou be the son of God. . . ." At his baptism had come the assurance that he was. Now comes the torturing doubt —perhaps he's not.

You have known this too. You have known peak days: A Sunday when the service seemed to fit your needs particularly and you went out uplifted and inspired; a family reunion, perhaps, when you could give hearty thanks to God for his goodness to you and yours; or an unforgettable moment on a mountaintop when the whole world stretched out at your feet and life was full of meaning and joy. You have had these peak days when you were on top of the world and faith in God came easily. But those peak days were always followed by Monday—blue Monday. Or it can be blue Tuesday or blue Thursday or blue every day, for that matter, when the trivial and the commonplace crowd in, when the drab and dreary routine of ordinary days all but smothers you with its dull sameness.

Can there be any doubt of it? The dangerous days for a man's faith, whether yours or our Lord's, are the dull, drab days. If there is a battle on our hands we can often enough manage it, because the blood is hot and there is a clear purpose ahead. Victory comes more readily then. Our nation at war, for example, was stronger than our nation is now in the ordinary days of peace.

Or when the days are really black, when death strikes someone close to you, and the load seems more than you can bear, you often stand amazed at the strength you find to endure suffering and grief. A man, even an ordinary man, frequently becomes heroic in a crisis.

This past winter, as in every winter, the papers carried the familiar stories of heroism. Somewhere a child fell through the ice again. And some ordinary, unheroic soul suddenly discovered a hero hidden inside of himself, and jumped in at the risk of his life to save the youngster. No one would have guessed, least of all themselves, that these ordinary people were heroes until the crisis came and demanded it. Days of crisis are not the most dangerous days for faith and courage. The peril lurks in the ordinary days when monotony and the commonplace stretch and yawn from dawn till dusk, days like the forty days in the wilderness, days when there is no ecstasy and no music, and when no extraordinary heroism is demanded of us. *Then* the temptation comes.

In the second place, I want you to notice how inevitable

it was. Jesus "was led up *of the Spirit* into the wilderness to be tempted." The Spirit which descended with its divine assurance upon Jesus in his baptism is the same Spirit which now drives him forth into the wilderness to be tempted. And is that, after all, so surprising? When Christ accepted for himself the call to be the chosen one of God he immediately risked the temptation to be less than that.

And this is true to our own experience too. We can avoid the peril of ordinary days by making sure that there are no extraordinary days. A man who refuses to set any high ideals for himself is never tempted to betray them. A man who is content to grovel along in life's lowlands, avoiding mountaintop experiences and never venturing a faith in God, will not know what I am talking about or what Jesus went through in the wilderness.

But once a man strikes hands with a high and lofty purpose in which he believes and to which he gives himself, he inevitably opens himself to the temptation to compromise and disillusionment. You have volunteered your time to canvass, let us say, for the community fund and had the door slammed in your face, figuratively and literally! There's the attempted kindness you've offered and it has been thrown back at you. And you begin to wonder whether it's worth it. So let's face it! It is inevitable. So long as there is evil in this world the man who decides to throw in his lot with God is going to face difficulties, frustrations, and heartaches. You are going to wonder whether God is real or not. You're going to ask, just as our Lord asked there in the wilderness, "Can this long, flat, dull, and dusty road of ordinary days lead me closer to God? This unheroic life of dirty dishes and crying children, of streetcars and time clocks, of telephone calls and ringing doorbells, of feeding the chickens and sweating for a week's pay—is this the life of a child of God?"

A lot of people think not, and imagine they can escape it. They run from movie to bar to roadhouse to marijuana to television to Miami to Reno to bingo and back to the movies again, hoping to escape the inevitable ordinary days. And as they run the devil just laughs. He knows there is no escape.

But he keeps trying to make you think there is! That was his strategy with Jesus in the wilderness. Each time the devil approached him, it was with the suggestion to try something startling and sensational to break the monotony of those days in the wilderness. "Change stones into bread," he whispered. "Throw yourself down from the pinnacle of the temple; you won't get hurt—*if* you are the Son of God—and think how the people will come running!" And then he tops these two with the most grandiose get-rich-quick scheme the world has ever seen. "Here," he said, "are all the kingdoms of the world—and they're all yours! All you have to do is admit I'm boss."

It was all a barefaced attempt to trap Jesus into thinking he could escape the ordinary days by resorting to excitement and the sensational. The devil even quoted Scripture to make it sound more convincing! But Jesus didn't fall into the trap. He knew that to do his Father's will he could not escape the ordinary days of life any more than you or I.

If you can go just this far, if you can accept the inevitability of the temptation in the wilderness, then half the battle is won. But how to meet the temptation when it comes? To recognize that every one of us is sure to experience periods of letdown in our spiritual lives and to expect them—that's half the battle. But it's only half. Watch how our Lord met the peril of ordinary days.

Notice that to the tempter's suggestion, "If you are the son of God . . . ," Jesus had no soul-shattering experience to assure him that he really was. No heavenly voice came, no spine-tingling vision. Rather, he met the tempter at every step of the road with a quotation from Scripture which no doubt he had learned by heart when he was a child: "Thou shalt not tempt the Lord thy God." Here in the wilderness there was no impassioned prayer to God such as he uttered in the garden on the night before he died. Here, calling upon a reservoir of habit built up through the years, he was simply obedient to what he knew of God. There was nothing else Jesus had to rely upon in all those dreary days except the old familiar guideposts, "Thou shalt not tempt . . . Thou shalt worship. . . ." Either Jesus could trust God and obey or he could fail to trust and disobey.

So with us. It is inevitable that we shall meet temptation in the wilderness of ordinary days. And the response then is not to look for some spine-tingling experience of the presence of God, which may or may not come, but rather to give expression to faith in simple acts of obedience. To reflect upon the will of God in Scripture. To say our prayers alone and together whether or not we feel like praying. To attend to our daily duties and chores whether or not they seem appropriate for a child of God. To give kindness whether or not people throw it back in our faces.

For mark this. It mattered not a bit how Jesus felt. Un-questionably he did not *feel* like the Son of God out there in the wilderness. He was tired, weak, hungry, and tormented by doubts, with no heavenly sign or divine assurance. He did not feel like the chosen one of God. But it didn't matter how he felt. He simply trusted and obeyed.

Nor does it matter how we feel. You will say that you don't feel very much like a child of God with your hands in the dishpan or up to your elbows in car grease. And I say that it doesn't matter how you feel. If religion were dependent upon how you feel, it would be full to the brim one moment and empty the next. And it would be empty precisely when you need it most! It doesn't matter how you feel, or what other people think about you, or even what you think about yourself. All that really matters is what God thinks of you. And if he thinks of us as his children then we ought to trust him as children and obey even if we don't always see where it's getting us.

And now—the issue of it all? "Angels came and ministered unto him." Light broke in upon the dull, ordinary days for our Lord in the wilderness. God, who had been with him all along, of course, now makes his presence known.

That is your assurance too. If it is inevitable that we shall be tempted in the dull and ordinary days and if it is required simply that we be found faithful and obedient in those days, it's not just a matter of blind obedience with nothing in store. The days are not all spent in the wilderness. God will make his presence known to you, too. There will again be days, peak days of song and inspiration, luminous hours when you will know that God is near and real. And the glory of them will rub off a little so that even the ordinary days will have the glint of God's presence upon them too.

Then Jesus went thence, and departed into the coasts of Tyre and Sidon. And, behold, a woman of Canaan came out of the same coasts, and cried unto him, saying, Have mercy on me, O Lord, thou Son of David: my daughter is grievously vexed with a devil. But he answered her not a word. And his disciples came and besought him, saying, Send her away; for she crieth after us. But he answered and said, I am not sent but unto the lost sheep of the house of Israel. Then came she and worshipped him, saying, Lord, help me. But he answered and said, It is not meet to take the children's bread, and to cast it to dogs. And she said, Truth, Lord: yet the dogs eat of the crumbs which fall from their masters' table. Then Jesus answered and said unto her, O woman, great is thy faith: be it unto thee even as thou wilt. And her daughter was made whole from that very hour.

Matthew 15:21-28

6.

+ + +

When God Is Deaf

Anyone who has ever tried to pray has come up against the embarrassing situation of apparently talking to a blank wall. God is deaf to our prayers. Or so it seems. People have prayed for fine weather and it has rained cats and dogs. They have prayed for health and been dogged all their days by chronic illness. They have prayed for the life of a loved one and even while the prayer was uttered, the loved one died. People have prayed for peace and wars have broken out all over the world. People have prayed for deliverance from tyranny and have suffered torture, imprisonment, and death.

Now, strangely enough, the Bible is full of examples of this same apparent deafness on the part of God. In the Psalms, that great devotional book of faith and praise, you run across passages like this: "O my God, I cry in the day-time, but thou answeredst not." Or this: "Be not silent unto me lest if thou be silent to me, I become like them that go down into the pit." Turn to the prophets and one of them starts right in with the complaint, "O Lord, how long shall I cry, and thou wilt not hear?" Or move over into the New Testament and you stumble over the same experience. Paul prays three times that his thorn in the flesh be removed but his prayer goes unanswered and for the rest of his life he has to make the best of it. Even Christ on the night before he dies prays in an agony that the cup of suffering and bitterness be removed, but shortly he rises from his prayer and drinks the cup to the dregs.

What shall we make of it, when God is deaf? At least we can start out by knowing that the experience is not common only to you and me, and that it is not necessarily an indication of lack of faith on our part. We can take comfort from the fact that the great spirits of the Old Testament, St. Paul, and even our Lord himself knew what it is like to pray and apparently have the prayer go unanswered.

Let us turn to the story of this woman of Canaan which is a kind of case history dealing with the problem of unanswered prayer. To her petition for help for her sick daughter, Jesus "answered her not a word." Why?

Well, in the first place, the woman was a stranger. Jesus had just left Judea and was traveling into a non-Jewish country where he had not been before. How did this woman come to know about him? Why had she come to this Jewish rabbi with her sick daughter? Stories, no doubt, had gone on ahead of him telling of his miraculous cures. Possibly she was at her wit's end trying any and every possibility to find a cure for her daughter. After all, what had she to lose?

And perhaps right there you will find one obvious answer to a lot of unanswered prayers. Is it too much to say that when in our extremity we turn to God for help we come, more often than we'd care to admit, as comparative strangers to him, getting around to prayer only when we don't know where else to turn, and then not bothering to pray until we are up against it again?

And have you ever thought what a mess this world would be if every prayer were answered? Just consider the spectacle of all sorts of people, many of whom are utter strangers to God and without the foggiest notion of what God wills or wants for this world, bombarding him with their various and often contradictory requests. Some of their requests are silly, some vain, some selfish, some even blasphemous, and all of them ignorant of their own profoundest needs. When you stop to think of it, the most merciful answer God can give to a whole host of our prayers is a gracious deafness. So Jesus, to this woman's first request for help, "answered her not a word." She was a stranger to him. And so, sometimes, are we.

But the woman persisted. She came and worshiped him, saying, "Lord, help me." And through her persistence she awakened a response. And that's the second thing we can learn from the story of this woman. You have to be prepared to prove your sincerity in prayer by your persistence, throwing your whole self after the prayer until the prayer becomes indeed your "soul's sincere desire."

And this means persistence not only in the asking but in thinking and working too. Prayer is no substitute for your own efforts. God is a father and he will no more do your own thinking and working for you than any father will do his boy's homework for him night after night. The father loves the boys and he could, presumably, work out his problems for him. But the father knows he should not if the boy is going to develop his own powers and character.

Very often, I suspect, when our prayers go unanswered we have failed here. We have failed to submit to the necessary discipline of thinking and working. Perhaps no single prayer which you and I have offered in the past few years has had so much of our heart in it as the prayer for a just and lasting peace. And what will come of it? Will God again seem to turn a deaf ear? Or will the answer depend upon the depth of our sincerity? Is God, perhaps, waiting for us to throw our whole selves after the prayer, heads and hands as well as hearts? There is not much sense in praying for peace while we look down our elegant noses at "inferior" races or sit down comfortably on top of the highest standard of living in the world with rarely a thought, much less a hand lifted, toward millions of people living on a bare subsistence level in Asia and Africa. No doubt God will, one day, answer the prayers of mankind for peace, when you and I and the rest of us prove with open hands and outgoing hearts that we really mean it and are willing to work and sacrifice for it.

So with this woman of Canaan. Her persistence brought a response. But it was not yet the response she wanted. To her continued pleading Jesus answered with a proverb, "It is not meet to take the children's bread and to cast it to dogs." And she answered, "Truth, Lord." Though the proverb does not sound as harsh in its original language as it does to us, it was still a rebuff. Yet there was an uncommon humility about this woman. She didn't grovel in front of Jesus to get what she wanted, nor did she whine and stand on her injured dignity when he tested her sincerity. She simply accepted herself for what she was, a nobody with no particular claim on anybody, least of all on Jesus.

Until you and I can accept ourselves and our difficulties with the same clear-eyed humility, we are going to have a lot of difficulty with unanswered prayer. Some of us, unlike this woman, think we have a claim on God. After all, we say, I go to church and say my prayers; I'm neighborly and lead a reasonably decent life; why shouldn't God grant just this one prayer of mine? Such a person wants reasons, not mercy. And God gives mercy, not reasons.

It may seem strange to you at first and yet if you think about it for a moment, I think you will agree that God cannot see life and its problems exactly as you and I see them. When you and I are faced with sorrow or suffering or difficulty, everything in our lives is colored by it. And although God sees what we are going through and understands what it means to us, his view of the world is not so colored. He sees our difficulty but he sees life—all of it— and thus sees our difficulty in its proper perspective. And what this woman of Canaan was doing was seeing her problem in perspective. "Truth, Lord." Even though she loved her daughter and wanted desperately to have her cured, her problem was not so important as some; she was not as worthy as some; she had no claim on Jesus at all. Yet, she persisted, there must be mercy even for such as me. And there was.

She came to Jesus convinced that he could help her and would respond to her prayer. I am lost in admiration for that little word, "yet." "Truth, Lord. Yet. . . ." It's a remarkable little word along with its oversize twin, "nevertheless." They keep ringing through the Bible like the sound of trumpets. There was Job, you remember, when everything had been taken from him except life itself, "Though he slay me, *yet* will I trust him." There was Peter after a long discouraging night's work with nothing to show for it, "We have toiled all the night and taken nothing, *nevertheless* . . . I will let down the nets." There was Christ on the night before he died, "If it be possible, let this cup pass from me, *nevertheless*, not my will but thine be done." This woman with her, "Truth, Lord. *Yet* . . ." belongs to a royal succession of those whose faith could not be shaken that God, or life, is basically good and that God will respond to that faith.

Notice that it was not a tentative "yet," not a "well, we'll give it one more try and see what happens" kind of thing. This woman of Canaan put her whole life and the life of her child into that little word "yet." So with Job and Peter and Christ. They threw their lives after their trust in God and he did not let them down.

The tragic thing is that when life gets us down and God apparently doesn't hear our prayers, we give in *too soon* to discouragement or despair. It's as if we stopped two-thirds of the way or nine-tenths of the way along the road; exactly as if this woman had given up after Jesus' first silence or after his rebuff. It's tragic because God never, *never* lets a man down who trusts him all the way. If you and I happen to read life otherwise, read our own particular difficulty or tragedy as evidence that God is not to be trusted any further, it's our reading of life, not his.

For the Christian reading of life is a triumphant affirmation that life is basically good because God is good; because God is faithful; because God is the God of Jesus Christ whose will for men is not failure and discouragement and despair, but whose will for us is victory and peace and joy. Those gallant souls, despite what life may be throwing at them at the moment—and I know at times it seems as if life were throwing the whole book at them—will trust that God will respond to their trust and will not let them down. "O woman, great is thy faith. Be it unto thee as thou wilt."

There is no guarantee that you will get exactly what you want. This woman did. She got the health of her child. Paul, on the other hand, still had his thorn in the flesh. Christ, for all of his prayer, still got a cross. And so may you.

But this same Christ is also your guarantee that God will never let you down. He will see you through to the end and beyond! When God seems to be deaf to your prayers, you can be assured that he is not. He is listening. And although the specific request you are making may not be within his power to grant, he will still answer you. He will respond to every prayer offered in persistent, humble faith. Not in the way you may expect or in the way that you may want, perhaps, but in the way that is best. You can trust him for that.

Come unto me, all ye that labour and are heavy laden, and I will give you rest. Take my yoke upon you, and learn of me; for I am meek and lowly in heart: and ye shall find rest unto your souls. For my yoke is easy, and my burden is light.

Matthew 11:28-30

7.

+ + +

When Religion Is a Burden

Have you ever reached the point when your religion became a burden? When the whole business seemed to be a dead weight on your shoulders and you wondered whether it was worth the struggle any longer? I have. And when it happens it's time to take it down and have a good long look at it because something has gone radically wrong with it.

There is no little irony in that striking passage in the Old Testament where the prophet of the Exile pictures the proud gods of Babylon, Bel and Nebo, being unceremoniously carted off in the face of danger. These dumb idols, these inert lumps of wood and stone, their noses in the dust, were supposed to save and protect. Now with the enemy at the gate they had to be hoisted laboriously to the shoulders of the faithful, loaded on to beasts of burden and carted off to safety. This is a vivid picture not only of the obvious ineptness of pagan idols but of every man's religion, even to the Christian's Christ, when, instead of uplifting and sustaining a man, it becomes no more than another piece of life's luggage that has to be carted along wherever he goes.

It was so in the time of Christ, certainly, when the religion of the Jews had become for most a ridiculously detailed observance of jots and tittles. A good Jew found himself picking his way through an incredible maze of six hundred-odd "thou shalts" and "thou shalt nots." The edge in this game of pious hopscotch went to the moneyed class for they had the leisure to work at it and become proficient. But for the poor it was no longer a "strong defense" or a "Lord's song"; it was a dead weight on their shoulders.

You would have thought that Christ had changed all that, but come down fifteen centuries and you find that the simplicities and lifting power of the gospel had been buried under a top-heavy superstructure of ecclesiastical complexities—just about as burdensome as that sounds!

And you would have thought that Luther and the reformers had changed all that, too, but here we are today and, as you look around at supposedly religious folk, it becomes painfully apparent that the Christian faith still bears a disturbing resemblance to Bel and Nebo, those Babylonian idols laboriously hoisted to the shoulders of the faithful, a dead weight to be carried instead of a saving and rejuvenating faith.

You ask a man why he joins the church. And more often than you would care to hear he will tell you, "Because it's a worthwhile community 'project' which deserves my 'support.'" If he's a man of broader vision he may even see it in terms of a necessary "prop" to shore up a beleaguered Western civilization. And so, like as not, he'll go on, "A man ought to 'get behind the church'; every good American ought to 'put his shoulder to the wheel' in these days of atheistic communism to keep the Christian church a going concern." The very phrases betray his basic attitude toward the Christian faith. It's a load to be carried, a project to be supported, or at least to be given a helpful shove along the way.

Although it is not the whole story by any means, so much of what you see when you look around inside the churches turns out to be a weary business of keeping a lot of creaking machinery going. Ask a man about his men's organization or the young people's society and, with some shining exceptions, chances are he will tell you a dreary story of pushing and pulling, of scratching heads and rubbing brains together in endless efforts at artificial respiration to breathe life into a corpse. And everyone knows how denominations have gone in for promotional secretaries by the bushel because the causes of the church will languish, apparently, unless they're constantly pushed and promoted.

I suppose it might be understandable if it were just a matter of organizational machinery. But this tendency creeps into the attitude toward worship too. It's habit, they will tell you, this going to church Sunday after Sunday. And it is, of course! But there's no light in their eye. It's a weekly chore, a duty to be discharged even if it wears them out.

Or look in on a university and find any number of fine young churchmen nursing their faith through college, worried that they won't be able to bring God alive through a survey course in sociology or contemporary philosophy. Indeed, some students find difficulty successfully nursing God through an introductory course in religion!

To be sure, all of these are no more than symptoms—superficial symptoms, perhaps—yet they suggest something radically wrong. They indicate that the Christian faith is under constant threat of betrayal into being a religion which depends upon man's efforts—your efforts!—the very thing for which it was supposed to be the answer. An idol that has to be carried.

Against this whole dreary setting of religion that has become a burden, I want you to listen to one of the most familiar sayings of Jesus: "Come unto me, all ye that labor and are heavy laden, and I will give you rest. Take my yoke upon you, and learn of me; for I am meek and lowly in heart: and ye shall find rest unto your souls. For my yoke is easy, and my burden is light." You have probably heard these words given a broader interpretation, but this great invitation was spoken in the first instance to those for whom religion was the burden.

"Come unto me, all ye that labor and are heavy laden with your *religion* and I will give you rest." That last phrase means, "I will refresh you." This is not the offer of an additional nap in the afternoon or the opportunity to put on your slippers and draw up by the fire. Rather is it the offer of new life and zest—a lift! That was the prophet's point back there by the waters of Babylon. Instead of dead, dumb idols which had to be loaded and hauled, he pointed to God and his everlasting arms. "I have made, I will carry," saith the Lord. It was Luther's point too. The Christian faith is not a matter of working at your religion but a new awareness of the God who is at work in you.

It is the heart of the gospel, the good news which takes a man's eyes off himself and his endless duties and failures and fixes them on God. God has been in this thing from the beginning. He doesn't intend to get out from under at this late date and lay the burden of it all on us. Although, frankly, I have often wondered why he doesn't! We have given him every justification to pull out and let us clean up the mess we have made of his world as best we can. But he won't! The cross is his eternal pledge and sign that, "I have made, I will carry."

This refreshment of soul which Christ offers us here, how do we get it? Note, in the first place, that Christ is at the center of it all, simply asking us to "come unto him" in love and trust. Try putting anything else at the center of religion except God and it turns out to be a burden every time—whether it's duty with its endless demands, or so many propositions in a creed to be accepted, or a church with its inevitable organizational machinery. Let these or anything else elbow Christ out of the center of religion and you have an idol on your hands—and it *is* on your hands quite literally, a burden to be hoisted and hauled.

But accept Christ's invitation to come unto him because he is at the center and religion is the refreshing and invigorating thing it promises to be. It's not unlike a boy and girl about to be married. There is a new relationship of love and trust at the center which gives zest and tang to their lives. They've got dreams and plans and they can hardly wait! Their jobs are not just jobs any longer because they now take on a new dimension of purpose. Their jobs mean something now: a house, furniture, and a future with bassinets and nurseries.

This is precisely the kind of refreshment Christ brings into the life of a man who accepts his invitation: a new beginning, a bracing of the shoulders for an exciting and creative enterprise. "Come unto me, all ye that labor and are heavy laden with your religion and I will refresh you." It will show! In your eyes, in your step, in the eagerness with which you tackle each duty the day offers.

But it's not just a lark, either. There is a yoke to be taken and a burden too. It is not a running away from responsibilities and duties, or an escape. Christianity never escapes anything! Neither death nor pain nor possible failure nor defeat. Don't let anyone try to tell you differently. The chores, the tasks, the demands are still there—only now they have been multiplied!

This must sound like nonsense. I started off by saying that if religion becomes a burden something is radically wrong with it. Now we are saying the demands upon the Christian are still there and multiplied. It sounds like double talk. But, you see, it all depends on what is at the center of it.

If we may return again for a moment to our starry-eyed young couple, they too are taking on new and bigger responsibilities. And even though shared, the responsibilities are multiplied by two at first, and as children come, by three and by four. But the added burdens are lighter even though greater because at the center is a relationship of love and trust. The "burden is light."

And the "yoke is easy," too, although not, perhaps, in the way we think. That phrase, the "yoke is easy," fairly smells of the farm country. Up in New Hampshire where we spend our summers you still occasionally run across a farmer driving a pair of oxen. You can almost hear him use the phrase in his deep New Hampshire accent, "That yoke sure rests easy on those oxen." It's easy, this yoke, because it fits.

It fits our situation with respect to sin. It takes full cognizance of the depth of our rebellion against God, the pride and pettiness inside each of us, looks steadily into our souls to see us exactly as we are, sees us in a way we are unwilling even to see for ourselves, and still says, "All right. Come and trust me anyway—just the way you are." And, speaking of burdens, what a weight that takes from our shoulders! You don't have to pretend any more—pretend that you're better than you really are (or worse!) since God certainly knows you're not! No need to play games any longer. God sees you for what you are and accepts you "as is." His yoke fits our situation with respect to sin.

And his yoke fits with respect to our potentiality for good, too. His love awakens us and calls forth our meager and tentative offerings of love in return in a way that no commands, no bribes, no threats, no punishment could ever do. It's strange, isn't it? Every parent with the barest portion of common sense knows that a child's conduct is at its best when he responds to love rather than to threat, or punishment, or bribe. Yet how reluctant we are to see that this is precisely the way the best Christian conduct comes about, not primarily because of divine rules and regulations, or because of fear of hell or promise of heaven, but simply because of God's amazing and undiscourageable love for the likes of you and me.

His yoke fits this mixture of sinners and potential saints that we are, this tragic jungle of good and evil which we call self. His yoke is "easy" because it fits! You and I are at home in this gospel as nowhere else in this world. And because at home, even though the demands are appalling in what they require of us—even to a cross—the "yoke is easy, the burden is light."

If your religion has become a burden for you, take it down and have a good long look—at the *center* of it. Because that is where the trouble lies. For religion is very much like falling in love. If you fall in love at the edges, with money or good looks, or out of a sense of responsibility, your marriage is headed straight for trouble because it is an intolerable burden. Fall in love with a person at the center, and the edges will pretty much take care of themselves. So with religion. Let the edges of it—duty, or creeds, or a church with its ceremonies and organizational machinery—elbow God out of the center of it and it is no better than Bel and Nebo, intolerable burdens to be hoisted and hauled. And heaven knows we've got enough burdens in life without piling religion on top of them! But fall in love with God at the center, and the edges of life, with the duties, the creeds, the ceremonies, and the machinery will pretty much take care of themselves.

A little boy once asked his father, "What does God do all day?" It's a good question. It's a good question to ask yourself whenever your religion threatens to become a burden. What *does* God do all day? The prophet had the answer, "I have made, I will carry." Christ said the same thing in more personal terms addressed directly to you: "Come unto me . . . and I will refresh you."

But whatever any one dares to boast of—I am speaking as a fool—I also dare to boast of that. Are they Hebrews? So am I. Are they Israelites? So am I. Are they descendants of Abraham? So am I. Are they servants of Christ? I am a better one—I am talking like a madman—with far greater labors, far more imprisonments, with countless beatings, and often near death. Five times I have received at the hands of the Jews the forty lashes less one. Three times I have been beaten with rods; once I was stoned. Three times I have been shipwrecked; a night and a day I have been adrift at sea; on frequent journeys, in danger from rivers, danger from robbers, danger from my own people, danger from Gentiles, danger in the city, danger in the wilderness, danger at sea, danger from false brethren; in toil and hardship, through many a sleepless night, in hunger and thirst, often without food, in cold and exposure. And, apart from other things, there is the daily pressure upon me of my anxiety for all the churches. Who is weak, and I am not weak? Who is made to fall, and I am not indignant? . . .

I must boast; there is nothing to be gained by it, but I will go on to visions and revelations of the Lord. I know a man in Christ who fourteen years ago was caught up to the third heaven—whether in the body or out of the body I do not know, God knows. And I know that this man was caught up into Paradise—whether in the body or out of the body I do not know, God knows—and he heard things that cannot be told, which man may not utter. On behalf of this man I will boast, but on my own behalf I will not boast, except of my weaknesses. Though if I wish to boast, I shall not be a fool, for I shall be speaking the truth. But I refrain from it, so that no one may think more of me than he sees in me or hears from me. And to keep me from being too elated by the abundance of revelations, a thorn was given me in the flesh, a messenger of Satan, to harass me, to keep me from being too elated. Three times I besought the Lord about this, that it should leave me; but he said to me, "My grace is sufficient for you, for my power is made perfect in weakness." I will all the more gladly boast of my weaknesses, that the power of Christ may rest upon me. For the sake of Christ, then, I am content with weaknesses, insults, hardships, persecutions, and calamities; for when I am weak, then I am strong.

II Corinthians 11:21b-29; 12:1-10 (RSV)

8.

+ + +

What Has Religion Done for You?

Have you ever sat down and asked yourself the question, "What, after all, has religion done for me?"

Before going any further, let me say emphatically that I know just how self-centered and crude that sounds. It conjures up the picture of a man standing before God demanding to know what God has ever done for him. It is a pretty low level on which to approach religion, I'll admit. And yet I want to approach religion on that level because it is precisely at that level that a lot of people are getting interested in religion these days. They are urged to come to church because they can leave their worries and troubles there. They are told that religion can help make them "healthy, wealthy, and wise." They are told that religion can help preserve the American way of life against the threat of communism. They are constantly being invited to examine religion on the basis of what they will get out of it.

Now the devilish thing about it—and I use the word "devilish" quite literally—is that there is a half-truth here. All of these things and more can very well be the *result* of religion. It is when they are made the *purpose* of it that the whole business gets dragged down to the level of its usefulness to you.

Rather than taking deliberate aim and letting fire with a broadside of arguments to blast this crude distortion of the Christian gospel with its literally blasphemous suggestion that God can be used to increase my own personal and private health, comfort, and security, let's play along with it at its own level. Let's play this game of examining what religion can do for you on its own field, using its own rules.

Let us turn, not to any vague generalities but to an actual bit of autobiography from the life of the Apostle Paul, of whose devotion to Christ there can be no question, and whose importance for the whole Christian enterprise is second only to that of our Lord. Paul sat himself down one day and answered out of his own experience this very question, "What has religion done for me?"

The occasion for it was a dispute in the church at Corinth where some had questioned Paul's authority in the church. Others had put forward claims that their right to lead the church was more valid than his. All right then, says Paul in effect, look here. I'll tell you what Christianity has done for me. If others boast about their qualifications, let me have "my little boast" too.

To begin with it is abundantly clear that religion, rather than keeping Paul out of trouble, got him into a whole mess of it. We don't have to catalogue every single item in the long list of trials and tribulations, but if ever you begin to think that life—or God, perhaps—has dealt harshly with you, take a look at Paul's experience.

It cost him hard work, of course. But beyond that there were floggings, not just one or two, but a half dozen of them. He was stoned, thrown into jail, shipwrecked; he suffered from cold and exposure and flirted constantly with death. All this and more not by chance or accident, we are led to presume, but directly as a result of his religious convictions.

Then beyond the physical sufferings went a suffering of mind and spirit too. What Paul did *not* get out of Christianity was peace of mind and soul in any shallow sense. There were sleepless nights. There came an added sensitivity to the plight of others: "Who is weak and I am not weak? Who is offended and I burn not?" There came additional burdens from the churches in his care. Instead of his religion getting him out from under, it actually pushed him under far more cares and responsibilities than he had ever had before. As if his own troubles were not enough he found himself loaded down with the problems of others.

So far, then, it seems that all Christianity did for Paul was to give him a singularly rough time of it: headaches, heartaches, and physical abuse. It suggests rather strongly that you and I may well expect religion to get us into trouble rather than out of it. Not that we have to go out and make martyrs of ourselves, of course. We don't have to go searching for the nearest bed of nails or crown of thorns just to prove to ourselves and to the rest of the world that we are faithful followers of Christ. To be sure, there are Christians in our own time who, like Paul, have been in prisons and in peril of death simply because they were faithful to their Christian convictions. The Nazis and Communists know them well. As for you and me, we may or may not be called upon for a similar witness. Circumstances will determine that. But at least we ought to expect Christianity to get us into trouble.

Someone has written that the Christian religion is a "storm in a golden frame." It occurs to me that the figure ought to be reversed. The storm is not at the center. The storm develops around the edges where God and his will come into contact with human life. The cross is the stormy reminder of what happens when God invades human life.

When a weather front of clear, cold, refreshing air moves down from Canada and hits a mass of hot, humid, stagnant air, storms develop along the edge of the cold front, often with lightning, thunder, and torrential rains. Even so does God's invasion of our world develop storms as it advances into the human scene. And insofar as you and I become in some measure agents or ambassadors of God in the world, we can expect a stormy time of it. If it does not bring actual physical suffering, as was the lot of Christ and Paul and so many of our contemporaries in Communist lands, it will at the very least bring a tortured conscience and increased sensitivity to the injustices done to others. A Christian cannot ever stand by and be a mere spectator to human suffering and misery without becoming more than a spectator, without entering in some degree into the misery and suffering himself and doing whatever may be done at the moment to alleviate some of it.

What has religion done for you? It has not made life easy for you. That's first. But that's not all.

Paul goes on in this autobiographical defense of himself to what he calls "visions and revelations of the Lord." He speaks in strange language here of being caught up into the "third heaven" and into "Paradise." Behind this strange language lay his experience of the immediate and present reality of God. If Christianity got him into a lot of trouble, it also gave him the assurance that God was near and real and vividly present to him.

You and I may never have such ecstatic visions and experiences. But as Christ has promised, you and I are not left comfortless either. We, too, are given the assurance not only that God cares for us but that he is present with us. It is well for us not to look too hard for any "feeling" of that presence. Our emotions can play strange tricks on us and we can make ourselves feel pretty much what we want ourselves to feel. Better to take our Lord at his word: "He that willeth to do my will shall know. . . ." Those who follow in obedience and trust will find God's reassuring presence along the way. This is the essence of faith. Not to look for a divine pat on the head or mysterious voices in the ear, but simply to follow God's will and we'll find that to be true which our Lord promised, "Lo, I am with you alway."

It is this assurance which gives point and purpose to the troubles and difficulties and added burdens. This is the golden core at the center about the edge of which the storms develop. Here lies not a superficial avoiding of worries and burdens but the deep and abiding joy which "no man taketh from you." Paul was kept going from shipwreck to flogging to prison, through sleepless nights and all the rest of it, by the tremendous assurance that it wasn't all futile, a beating of the fists against the iron bars of an implacable fate, but that God was in it too, working out his eternal purpose of love—through him.

Bishop Lilje, writing of his experiences in a Nazi prison camp, tells of this strange assurance that came to him when he was brought to trial. "I was interested to notice that the officials of the law courts and of the Special Police continually looked uneasily in the direction of the representatives of the [Gestapo]! Here again, everything seemed upside down. We, whose fate was actually decided when we entered this building, were essentially more independent and more free than they were; the slaves were not in *our* ranks!" [1] And Christianity can give you that amazing assurance. It can do *that* for you. It may already have done that for you. It will get you into trouble—no doubt about that! But there will be the assurance that life has purpose and direction, that joy and love and freedom are at the heart of things, a peace of God which does indeed pass all understanding, a golden core framed by storms!

But there's one thing more Paul brings into his account of what religion had done for him. It revolves around that "thorn in the flesh" which he prayed three times to have removed. We don't know what it was, this "thorn in the flesh," possibly a physical infirmity of some kind or a chronic disease, perhaps. We do know that it plagued him constantly and that it kept him humble. He says so himself. It was this "thorn in the flesh" which kept him aware that he was constantly dependent not upon himself and his considerable gifts and talents but upon God's strength and mercy.

[1] Hanns Lilje, *The Valley of the Shadow* (Philadelphia: Muhlenberg Press, 1950), p. 97.

This is an important point. It means that for all Paul suffered and for all his assurance that God had been with him every moment of it, he realized that he did not have God at his beck and call. This is the great temptation for the religious man. Just because his faith has led him into difficulties and just because he has felt the assurance of God's presence he may jump to the conclusion that he has found the secret clue which enables him to put God at the end of a string and make him jump when he wants something. Like all ministers I get any number of pamphlets from various sources which declare that someone has discovered the "secret" of spiritual power, of health, of happiness, prosperity, and security. And every time it turns out to be this same spiritual monster: the man who thinks he has God at the end of a string.

Not so for Paul. Religion gave him a thorn in the flesh to keep him humble. And I suspect that you and I have some such thorn in the flesh too, if we have the grace to see it. It may be a physical infirmity. Or it may be some nagging temptation which never seems to leave us alone: lust, perhaps, or a driving ambition, or impatience with others, or a well-nursed grudge, or simply the realization that we have done so little with what God has given to us. Whatever it may be, it is there and if recognized pulls us down to a humble recognition that whatever God may have accomplished through us is his doing, not ours.

What, then, has religion done for you? This is what it did for Paul: It got him into trouble; it gave meaning, purpose, and joy to his life; and it left him with a thorn in the flesh to keep him humble before God. That's the record. I grant you it would have been more pleasant simply to tell you about the golden core and forget the storms and the thorn. But occasionally it is well to keep the record straight and see the whole truth, not just the part of it we like to hear. And if we are going to sell Christianity on the basis of what it can do for you, then we had best keep in mind *all* that it will do for you. Someone once put it this way: Christ did not come to make life easy; he came to make men great. And religion *can* do that for you!

PART III

+ + +

"As strangers and pilgrims . . . "

When the unclean spirit is gone out of a man, he walketh through dry places, seeking rest; and finding none, he saith, I will return unto my house whence I came out. And when he cometh, he findeth it swept and garnished. Then goeth he, and taketh to him seven other spirits more wicked than himself; and they enter in, and dwell there: and the last state of that man is worse than the first.

Luke 11:24-26

9

+ + +

The Empty House

Have you ever been in an empty house? No matter how striking or attractive it may appear on the outside, it's a forlorn thing inside. As you walk through it your footsteps leave hollow echoes ringing through the cold and empty rooms and you feel that the house is dragging out its meaningless existence, waiting for life and warmth to move in again. But an empty house never remains completely empty for long. Spiders move in to spin their webs; mice gnaw their way through the baseboards; rats scurry behind the wainscoting; bats flutter ominously in the attic.

Jesus uses this dramatic figure of the empty house in a weird kind of story which lays its finger on the peril of an empty soul. Using the popular belief in demons as a setting, he presses the point home. A demon, expelled from a man's soul, wanders through "dry places," the desert wastes, and ruins, where these unpleasant creatures like to spend their vacations. This demon, however, finds nothing to his liking in the desert wastes and decides to return to the life from which he has been banished. To his delight he finds it "swept and garnished," all cleaned up and decorated—and empty. Immediately he rounds up seven other horrible friends of his and takes possession once more, this time in force. For it is infinitely more difficult to evict eight tenants than one. So Jesus observes grimly, "The last state of that man is worse than the first."

It is a weird kind of parable but it cuts like a surgeon's knife to lay bare the vast, aching emptiness of our times. For the soul of our world is for the most part an empty soul. Those who diagnose the ills of our day agree on this with amazing uniformity. They all agree that something is wrong but the something wrong almost inevitably turns out to be something missing, an emptiness rather than some specific evil which ought to be rooted out.

Time, for example, in discussing the young people of today, has labeled them the "silent generation." Alan Walker, following a visit to a number of American campuses with the University Christian Mission, comments: "No doubt the silence is in part a reflection of confusion and bewilderment. After all this is the generation that . . . was born during the depression, went to grade and high school during the second world war, and now is at college during the bitter 'cold war' with Russia. . . . Youth shares with this whole generation the absence of confident answers to the problems of our times, and being unsure as to what must be done, often is silent." That silence becomes more ominous when, as happened not long ago, college students preferred to keep silent rather than take part in a formal debate on a controversial issue for fear someone might misunderstand and label them subversive. When young people are afraid to speak their minds it's not only an unhealthy sign for the future of democracy in this country, it also betrays an emptiness, a lack of courage and conviction in their souls.

Or here is Liston Pope, Dean of the Yale Divinity School, in an article with the significant title, "Vacuum on the Left": "There have been few times in American history, if any, when the note of social protest was as faint as it is at present. . . . The territory left of center is almost devoid of occupants." [1] It's true. All over the country men are afraid to speak out any longer for progressive ideas and goals. There is a growing vacuum on the left.

Or here is Kermit Eby writing of the labor movement: "The majority of union members want the protection of their unions, but do not want to bother to go to meetings to determine its policies. . . . The issues are complex; the experts know the answers. Let the experts fix things up and we'll drop in at a bar or go home and watch television." There is an emptiness there, too.

Moreover, many businessmen I know are unhappy, bewailing the lack of incentive due to big government and prohibitive taxes. Again the problem is a lack, an emptiness.

And so we could go on. Wherever you look, the documentation is impressive that if there is a crisis in our times it is a crisis of emptiness. Our Western world bears a disturbing resemblance to the empty house Jesus described. It is swept clean of demons, for have we not swept out superstition with universal education? Have we not swept our world clean of the demons Kaiser Wilhelm and Hitler and Mussolini and Hirohito? And are we not keeping the broom going with armaments and congressional investigations to keep the house clean of the demon communism?

[1] *Christianity and Crisis*, XI (August 6, 1951), p. 105.

The Empty House

The house is swept clean and garnished—how entrancingly garnished!—with sleek airliners, television, atomic power, new and flashier cars every year, with bright modern buildings of glass and stainless steel, with plastics and nylons and everything, even pot roasts and peanuts, wrapped up in cellophane. The house sparkles and glitters but the footsteps within have an ominously hollow sound.

Swept, garnished and—empty, seven other demons more wicked than the first threaten constantly to move in and take over: fear, hysteria, the political demagogue, confusion, futility, and with them come their "sisters and their cousins and their aunts," corruption, delinquency, narcotics, and alcohol, those trusty camp followers sucking the virtue and vitality out of a nation's morals. And the last state of that man may well be worse than the first.

The answer? The answer to it all is so obvious that Jesus did not bother to put it into words. He was the answer. He, telling the story, embodied the answer to the desolation of the empty house, the empty soul. And no one today seriously denies the validity of his answer. The aching void in our world is fairly crying for religion, for the Christian religion, for Christ. No doubt you are nodding your head right now in agreement. And so, having done our duty, you and I, by analyzing the situation and prescribing the proper remedy for the empty house, we go off wagging our heads wondering why more people don't see it as clearly as we do.

What we tend to forget is that, as Christ embodied the answer in the first century, you and I must embody the answer to our world in the twentieth century. If the answer to the emptiness of our times is God, then lives—your life and my life—in which God has filled the emptiness are the only means by which the answer can be communicated to the world. Bluntly, if this is the answer, you and I who talk about the answer must do more than talk; we must *be* the answer.

But that puts quite a different complexion on the matter, doesn't it? It's very easy to talk about God being the answer to our world until we stop and realize that the only way God can be the answer is through people like you and me. A lot of us have never really taken our religion with quite that kind of abandon. We are perfectly willing to take God into the house of our soul as a tenant—but only with proper reservations.

Our attitude is not unlike that of the cautious landlord who looks over his prospective tenants with a wary eye and reads them the house rules in order to avoid any future difficulties or misunderstandings: no pets, no children, quiet after 9:30 at night, no raucous parties. The landlord makes it quite plain that he wants decent, quiet, respectable tenants who will cause him no discomfort or disturbance.

So our cautious Christian views God as a prospective tenant: I welcome him into the house of my soul, of course, so long as he observes my house rules. I want it understood that I want no discomfort or disturbance in the way I run my life. I don't want to change my habits; if I have a few prejudices I don't intend to change them. I shall expect a reasonable amount of "peace of mind"; I don't want to lie awake nights worrying about the problems of the world or the state of my own soul; I have worries enough as it is. If God wants to move into my house under those conditions, I'll be more than happy to have him as a tenant and will, on my part, do what I can to make his stay with me agreeable. I'll go to church when the weather's fine and I'm not too busy or otherwise engaged, and say my prayers, and do what I can to practice the Golden Rule.

And I suppose some would be utterly amazed to learn that God never did move in under those terms or any other terms. Those who offered those terms thought they had a decent tenant in the house, but the house was actually empty all the time except for all the demons who moved in quietly and unobserved.

For, as C. S. Lewis has suggested, when God does come as a tenant into an empty house he doesn't act at all like the nice, quiet tenant you bargained for. "At first, perhaps, you can understand what He's doing. He's getting the drains right and stopping the leaks in the roof and so on; you knew that these jobs needed doing and so you are not surprised. But presently he starts knocking the house about in a way that hurts abominably and which doesn't seem to make sense. . . . [Actually] He is building quite a different house from the one you thought of—throwing out a new wing here, putting on an extra floor there, running up towers, making courtyards. You thought you were going to be made into a decent little cottage: but He is building a *palace*." [2] In fact, he acts as if he owned the place and before long you can hardly call your life your own. And as a matter of fact you can't. Because, you see, he intends to come and live there forever. It's no longer your house. It's his.

Of course God is the answer to the aching void, the

[2] C. S. Lewis, *Beyond Personality* (New York: Macmillan Co., 1945), p. 49.

emptiness which lies under the glittering surface of our world. But how can the world know the answer unless you and I give evidence in lives of quiet confidence and joy and love that the houses of our souls are not empty too, that God has in fact taken over so that we can no longer call our souls our own?

Some time ago *Life* published a picture of "The little boy who wouldn't smile." It was the gaunt, drawn, hungry face with staring, empty eyes of a little Korean boy named Kang Koo Ri who was found by an army chaplain huddled over his mother's dead body. He represented, of course, millions of homeless, hungry, empty children in a dozen countries who need our help. About a year later *Life* came out with a picture of little Kang Koo Ri, fat-faced and smiling. He had been brought to a Christian orphanage where he received food and love.

Those two pictures are a very live symbol of the change that can take place on the face of our world when the answer to the emptiness of our times finds expression in lives like ours that are filled with God, his joy, and his love. The change cannot take place overnight. It happens one by one. It will be slow, heartbreakingly slow at times. But it can and does happen. And when it does happen it has no other place to start except with you.

Now the word of the Lord came to Jonah the son of Amittai, saying, "Arise, go to Nineveh, that great city, and cry against it. . . ."

Jonah 1:1-2a (RSV)

10.

+ + +

The Reluctant Prophet

Among fishermen, the story of the big one that got away is commonplace. But the story in reverse of the *man* who got himself hooked by a whopping big fish and got away— that's news! For a good many people that's about all the news the little book of Jonah has ever had for them. And that's a pity, because if we can get past the incredible picture of Jonah in the belly of a whale, for a moment, we will find that this little book is as up to date as tomorrow's newspaper.

The book, of course, is a parable, not history. We don't know who the author was. Some time after the return from the exile the people of Israel, hardened rather than chastened by that harrowing experience, were turning in upon themselves as the only people in the world upon whom God could possibly look with favor. In that period one dauntless and farsighted soul wrote this story of Jonah, the reluctant prophet.

The story begins innocently enough, with the word of God coming to Jonah to "arise and go to Nineveh, that great city, and cry against it for their wickedness has come up before me." Surely a reasonable request to ask of any of God's prophets. But Jonah's reaction is peculiar. He runs away; gets himself down to a handy seaport and hops a boat for Spain.

Why did Jonah run away? To preach God's judgment upon the Assyrians, the ancient and implacable enemy of the Jews, for whom Jonah certainly had no sympathy, was not an uncongenial task. I suppose someone will suggest that Jonah may have been afraid. After all, if the word of God came to you today to arise and go to Moscow and cry against it because of its wickedness, you might think twice about it too and perhaps hop a boat for the Hawaiian Islands instead. But Jonah was no coward, as we shall see.

The reason Jonah ran away was because Jonah *was* afraid—not of what might happen to him, but of what might happen to the people of Nineveh. He was afraid they might repent and God, instead of punishing them, would forgive them. If Jonah had been sure that God would stick to his justice and the inevitable punishment of evildoers like the Assyrians, no doubt he would have gone. But he didn't trust God's love. It was apt to forgive the wrong people! And so he ran away. Jonah should have known better, of course. He went on board ship, climbed into his bunk and fell asleep. But God caught up with him in a storm at sea. And the frantic sailors and their captain, fearing for their lives, woke him up, suspecting that Jonah was the cause of it all. And he was.

You can't escape from God; it seems silly to try. He always does catch up with us sooner or later in some storm of life, whether it be a civilization, a nation or an individual like you or me. You only have to look back a few decades to see it on the broad stage of Western civilization. Scientists were going merrily about their research, probing into the secrets of electronics and energy, soberly declaring that their responsibility was limited only to research and discovery, not to the moral consequences of what the rest of us did with their discoveries. And the rest of us stood around and nodded agreement. Research is one thing and what happens as a result of it is quite another. Nothing must interfere with the scientific conscience in its search for "truth," for somehow, some way, good will come of it. So it went in our world until a cloud, somewhat larger than a man's hand, appeared over the horizon in the shape of a mushroom and Hiroshima lay in ruins. And suddenly they were not merely enemy Japanese, those 100,000 burned and twisted bodies, they were persons with names. And, strangely, we felt guilty. God had caught up with our flight into the ivory tower of scientific progress whence only good can come!

Or look at the nations. They too were going merrily about their business of exploiting the riches and cheap labor of Africa, India, China, and the exotic and fabulous lands and islands of the South Seas until the storm came and now whole continents are in revolt against white empires built on colonialism with its double standard of values for white and colored. The Communist threat in those areas, dangerous as it may be, must not blind us to the deeper motivation behind this large-scale revolution on the part of the colored peoples of the world. God has caught up with us Christian white people in the storm over Asia and Africa. There is no escape from God. You know it and so do I. And so did Jonah!

For Jonah it came in the peril to the lives of these pagan sailors, these pagans whom Jonah had come to despise because they were constantly at odds with God's people, raiding their villages, carting off half the population into captivity, and forever tempting them to forsake or water down the faith that had been handed down to them by Abraham and the prophets. But now in the crisis of the storm at sea threatening their lives, they were for Jonah no longer pagans, but persons. They were men like himself, with lives to live, with wives and children at home facing bereavement, persons capable of dreams and sympathy, even heroism! For when Jonah offered to throw himself overboard to calm the storm, these pagan sailors would have none of it but rowed all the harder in a vain attempt to bring the ship to land to save Jonah as well as themselves.

What a picture—2300 years old!—of the classic answer to prejudice and exclusiveness. Put a Negro Protestant, a white Catholic, a Jew—and yourself—on a raft somewhere in the Pacific and the racial and religious prejudices break down as the crisis of survival shakes men down to their common humanity. So Jonah, his unrelenting hatred of the pagans broken by the realization that these sailors were human beings like himself, had himself thrown overboard to save their lives.

If that had been the end of Jonah, no doubt seaports all over the world would be dotted with little Jonah Chapels dedicated to the brave Hebrew prophet who gave his life to save the lives of those pagan sailors. But this was not the end of Jonah. God still had Nineveh and its wickedness on his hands. And God was not through with Jonah either.

So enters the "great fish" whom God appointed to "swallow up Jonah" and to cast him up a little later on the shore. This incident of the great fish indicates that God's purpose is never completely thwarted. In the history of Israel, the exile in Babylon seemed to mean the end of God's purpose for his chosen people, just as Jonah's going overboard seemed to mean the end of God's purpose for Nineveh. But after the dark days of exile the people were returned to their land, thrown up on the shore again, so that God's ultimate purpose might be effected in the coming of our Lord.

So with Jonah. The reluctant prophet had been brought to the point where he had been willing to change his mind and accept God's point of view with respect to a few pagans. But the question whether his ingrained narrow religious horizons, his hatred of the Assyrians as a people had been overcome, was still not resolved.

You know how it is with us. There are levels of prejudice like everything else. You and I can reach the level where we say we will take each individual, of whatever race, creed, or political persuasion, and let him prove himself on his own merits, and then take great unction to ourselves for our broad-mindedness! And this is a step in the right direction. But is this the whole mind of God in the matter? The very fact that we start with the presupposition that each individual has to prove his worth to us first, indicates that we may be something more than reluctant to believe the best about others as a group. And God is not through with Jonah or with us, either, until we are "transformed," as Paul puts it, by the "renewing of our

minds," until those minds of ours become as large in their
sympathies as God's.

So again God's call came to Jonah to "go up to Nineveh,
that great city, and cry against it" for its wickedness. This
time Jonah went, preaching destruction within forty days
unless the city repented. And what a preacher he must
have been, this reluctant prophet! Not even Billy Graham
has done as well. Everyone from the king on down put on
sackcloth and ashes in the hope that God would relent.
And God did relent and forgave Nineveh its wickedness.

But Jonah was anything but pleased with the success of
his preaching! What he had feared from the very beginning had happened. God's love was not to be trusted. It
went too far. It included everyone, even the enemies of
God and his people. It lacked discrimination, this love of
God; it had no taste. Apparently it could not tell the difference between right and wrong, between good people
and bad. So Jonah went out of the city and sulked, his
bitterness at God increased by a flaming sun beating down
and a hot desert wind. So God took pity and had a plant
grow up to shade Jonah's head. And like all of us when
we're out of sorts, if we get physically comfortable, life
does not seem quite so unbearable as it did before. But the
next day God had a caterpillar destroy the plant and in the
heat of the sun Jonah's bitterness returned and he finally
blurted out that he was angry enough to die. Whereupon
God prodded Jonah gently, "Do you do well to be angry,
Jonah? You spend your pity on this poor withered plant
for which you have had no responsibility at all. Should not
I pity those ignorant and confused thousands of people in
Nineveh?" That is how this story ends: with pagan Nineveh

repentant and forgiven and Jonah, man of God, squatting on his haunches outside the city, enjoying the sulks.

What shall we make of it? Is it so difficult for us to understand Jonah's attitude here at the end? Surely there's many a man who is sulking outside the church today, bitter because God did not act in his life the way he thought God ought to have acted.

But what of us within the churches? We, too, are always open to the peril that, just because we are good religious people, others may be considered not quite as good as we are—even potentially. Else why do churches pick up and move out—"relocate" is the fashionable word for it; run away is more accurate—because the neighborhood has become "undersirable"? The people are still there. Is it that even potentially they are not worth our time and patience?

Or turn it around and look out at the troubled affairs of nations these days. Why is it that the churches with one voice urged the government to seek negotiation with Red China over the Formosa issue rather than throw down the military gauntlet? Was it not in the hope that in all men there is at least a potentiality for good to which we can appeal, and to which we must appeal so long as that possibility is open to us? It's the Jonahs of our time who want to throw bombs first and ask questions afterward.

But there is more than the temptation to think of others different from ourselves in color, creed, or political persuasion as of a lower order, even potentially. There is the constant peril for religious people to think they can make God fit their own narrow little minds instead of stretching their minds to the measure of God's mind. And never is this peril greater than among people of some religious maturity who know a bit about what they believe and why. The devil has a nasty habit of always climbing up to the higher levels of life with us. There *is* strength in knowing what you believe and sticking to it! But the devil is right at your elbow insinuating that this must be the only way God thinks too! And before long the devil has us convinced that we have God all neatly tucked away in our vest pocket. And from there it is an easy matter to start manipulating God's love and judgment, deciding who shall and who shall not be saved, and determining whether this group or that is actually worth our time and patience.

Do you remember how it was with our Lord? His biggest problem was not with the riffraff, the sinners, the adulterers, and social outcasts. He often found them to be the very best people—potentially! His biggest problem was with the good, decent, church people who rejected him because they wanted to keep God down to a manageable size—their size! Christ's love, too, lacked discrimination and taste; it could scarcely tell right from wrong, good people from bad!

The tragedy of Jonah is not that the reluctant prophet may, for all we know, still be squatting on his haunches outside of Nineveh sulking because his mind refused to grow up to the dimensions of God's mind. The tragedy is that after 2300 years, with God's mind meanwhile having been made perfectly clear for us in the crucified and risen Christ, you and I are still tempted to be reluctant prophets like Jonah. We wonder perhaps whether God can actually find anything really worth loving in the Red Chinese jet pilot, the Russian Communist spy, the East African Mau Mau, or some undesirables closer to home! Whereas God goes on the grand assumption that within every man—white Protestant American, yellow Chinese Red, black South African—is the capacity to respond to his love! This is the mind of Christ: That God is always eager to believe the best about the worst; that he is eager to believe the best despite the worst in all of us! So Paul writes, "Let this mind be in you." God grant that it may.

For it will be as when a man going on a journey called his servants and entrusted to them his property; to one he gave five talents, to another two, to another one, to each according to his ability. Then he went away. He who had received the five talents went at once and traded with them; and he made five talents more. So too, he who had the two talents made two talents more. But he who had received the one talent, went and dug in the ground and hid his master's money. Now after a long time the master of those servants came and settled accounts with them. And he who had received the five talents came forward, bringing five talents more, saying, "Master, you delivered to me five talents; here I have made five talents more." His master said to him, "Well done, good and faithful servant; you have been faithful over a little, I will set you over much; enter into the joy of your master." And he also who had the two talents came forward, saying, "Master, you delivered to me two talents; here I have made two talents more." His master said to him, "Well done, good and faithful servant; you have been faithful over a little, I will set you over much; enter into the joy of your master." He also who had received the one talent came forward, saying, "Master, I knew you to be a hard man, reaping where you did not sow, and gathering where you did not winnow; so I was afraid, and I went and hid your talent in the ground. Here you have what is yours." But his master answered him, "You wicked and slothful servant! You knew that I reap where I have not sowed, and gather where I have not winnowed? Then you ought to have invested my money with the bankers, and at my coming I should have received what was my own with interest. So take the talent from him, and give it to him who has the ten talents. For to every one who has will more be given, and he will have abundance; but from him who has not, even what he has will be taken away. And cast the worthless servant into the outer darkness; there men will weep and gnash their teeth."

Matthew 25:14-30 (RSV)

11.

+ + +

The One Talent Man

One of the curious facts about the Christian faith is that the biggest stumbling block in the way of our acceptance of it is not so much what we believe or don't believe about God, but rather what we believe about ourselves.

And that is why I'd like to turn to one of the most familiar of the parables of Jesus, the parable of the talents. It is a simple story and yet, like most simple things, the longer you look at it the more questions it raises. And chief among the questions is this: Why is it that Jesus puts the one talent man on the spot? For no matter where you swing the spotlight over the story of the talents, it inevitably is drawn to this little man, cowering there before his master offering up his one talent all safe and sound.

And the question persists: Why did our Lord single out the one talent man for his scathing rebuke? He could just as well have told the story so that the five talent man could have been the object lesson, and you and I, ordinary one talent people, would have sat back and enjoyed the story so much the more. For who does not get a kind of unholy pleasure in seeing Jesus cut the Pharisee down to size or with his quick wit leave the chief priests mumbling in their beards? But not here. Here he picks on this poor fellow who had so very little to begin with.

It is particularly curious in view of Christ's usually sympathetic concern for the lone individual who had little to offer except that he was "lost" or a "sinner." It's the little, overlooked, and outcast individual who is almost invariably the hero of his other stories: a despised Samaritan, a wastrel son in a pigsty, a beggar named Lazarus. Why then the withering scorn with which he pictures this poor, cautious, fearful little man? After all, he had done nothing dishonest. He had simply done what most people did in those days to keep money safe. He'd dug a hole in the ground and buried it; and then when the master returned, he dug it up again and gave it back: "Here you have what is yours." He wasn't an evil or a selfish man. Why does Christ point the finger at him?

Actually it is precisely because of our Lord's great and constant concern for the little, apparently unimportant people and what we consider the insignificant things in life that he turns the spotlight on the one talent man. It is all part of his indefatigable campaign to reverse our ordinary scale of values.

Here we are, you and I, forever being hypnotized by the busy and important affairs of the world, with an insatiable appetite for size and bigness: the biggest airplane, the biggest city, the biggest bomb, the biggest steel plant, the newspaper with the biggest circulation, the biggest hospital, the biggest congregation in town. If it's big, we figure, it must be an indication of some unusual worth or value.

So our Lord, in contrast, is forever picking out some

insignificant detail and making *that* important: five loaves
and two fishes—two *small* fishes—among five thousand; the
tiniest seed he could think of, a mustard seed; the smallest
coin in circulation, a widow's mite; a lily, a sparrow, a
pinch of salt. All this to accustom our eyes to a new way
of looking at things; that size and bigness are often enough
a delusion and a snare, and the small and insignificant are
loaded with possibilities.

And what is true in the world of things is true in the
world of people. You and I no longer measure a man by
the size of his salary, I hope; we have enough sense for that.
But if not by the size of his salary and his bank account,
then certainly a man is measured by the amount of responsibility he carries. Is this not a perfectly valid test by which
to measure a man's worth and importance? He's a big man
if he holds down a big, responsible job, directing the
affairs of many people or managing large sums of money.

And yet notice how God works: Not in the center of the
world's stage but off in a corner where you'd least expect
him. First he chooses an obscure little nomadic tribe and
promises them, of all people, his care. Then later he sends
his Son, not into the center of things, but into an off
corner of the world, born not even in a decent bed but in
a stable in a tiny village; has him grow up like a peasant,
not even in the center of that little country but in a back
country district with a peculiar accent all its own; and
finally has him buried in a borrowed tomb.

And this Son of his continues this same unrelieved
emphasis upon the small and insignificant, shunning the
big and important people, the five talent men who, as in the
story, are perfectly capable of taking care of themselves,

and making friends with the oddest lot of unpromising souls you ever saw: a woman taken in adultery, a blind beggar along the roadside, and that ridiculous and impossible little man up a tree, Zacchaeus. And all of this to get us adjusted to this quite incredible idea that God is tremendously concerned about little ordinary people—about you and me!

So perhaps it's not so difficult to understand why the spotlight in the story is kept focused on the one talent man. That apparently is right in character. But it still doesn't answer the question why Jesus is so hard on the poor fellow in the parable.

And the answer to that, I think, lies here. There are peculiar perils lying in wait for the five talent man, the man of unusual opportunities and responsibilities—the perils of becoming smug, indifferent, aloof and loveless. But the one talent man is beset by his own peculiar perils too. Chief among them is that he is far too ready to think of himself as a little man, of no great importance to anybody, not even to God. He is the man with only one vote, so why bother? He is the anonymous city dweller who can wander from the straight and narrow with no one the wiser, so why not wander? He is the man on the assembly line or the clerk in the big office, replaceable as a flat tire. He is the small stockholder in the big corporation whose sole responsibility is to cash his dividend check. He is the man who never makes the newspapers unless he dies or bites a dog. He is the occasional attender at church who prudently keeps the door open just a little for God, but avoids all the responsibility in church or community that he decently can because someone else will do it if he doesn't.

And it was this cringing self-debasement, this hiding behind the skirts of his littleness, which caused our Lord to blaze away at him in anger: "Thou wicked and slothful servant!" God was concerned about him, had risked everything for him, and he stands there cowering, not trusting God enough to make use of what God had given him.

And yet the fact of the matter is that God is accustomed to working wonders with little one talent people who have faith enough in Him to have some faith in themselves and their significance! Rip the haloes off the heroes and saints of the past. Take a look at them "before the halo": Moses —a man with blood on his hands and a stammer in his tongue; James and John—loud-mouthed fishermen blustering about what big shots they were going to be in the kingdom of God; Peter—a blundering hulk of a man with his foot in his mouth half the time; Paul—an unimpressive and bitter little Pharisee biting and snapping at the heels of the earliest Christians. Stand them up here without their haloes, these little one talent men whose one talent God took and twisted into a halo, so that today we call them saints!

So it has gone even today, these little people, laughing-stock of the world, who are remarkable for only one thing. They did not, like this little man in the parable, go cowering along shrugging off their daily opportunities and responsibilities while they whined about the way things were going in the world. They had taken whatever God had placed in their hands, however unpromising it might have appeared, trusting only that somehow God would make something of it. And God *has* made something of it, a movement which has changed the history of the world, not once, but a dozen times, and which will still be at it when communism and its world-wide conspiracy and the American way of life with its Coca Cola and television are items in some future encyclopedia of ancient and extinct cultures.

You now! With that one talent of yours—or perhaps it's two! The spotlight shifts from this fearful, cautious little man in the parable and turns its glare on you. Naturally, it would be more convenient if *we* could work the spotlight. We'd shift it in a hurry and, like the covers of *Time*, keep it trained on the five talent men where it belongs: on Eisenhower and Churchill and Dulles and Adenauer and what God might get done in his world through the likes of them! But God handles the spotlight despite our feeble, fluttery protests about how we're really not very much; he keeps turning it back on you! He wants to know what you've done and what you're doing now with your God-given opportunities.

The fact of the matter is, if we take this parable seriously and the man who told it, all heaven—quite literally!—all heaven is in a sense breathless at this moment, watching on tiptoe, wondering about you and what kind of a person you are turning out to be.

You don't believe it? That's not surprising. The Bible always did say that unbelief is the greatest of sins. And the greatest obstacle to faith is not whether God is personal or not; not whether he is a God of love or not; not whether Jesus of Nazareth is really divine or only a good man. These questions are not the crucial ones because they can be debated without any personal involvement on our part. This is the crucial question, this is the obstacle: to believe that all heaven is tremendously concerned about **you**.

To be sure this does not strike us as being too strange

when we apply it to somebody else: when a whole community turns out to look for a child who has wandered off into the woods; or when the community stands at the entrance to a mine shaft waiting for word about that one miner caught in a cave-in down below; or when a whole country picks up its morning newspaper with the prayer that that one kidnapped child has been found safe. That we can accept, that we should be concerned about the welfare of one lone individual who is somebody else. But that's not the point. The point is that this same concern—on a divine scale—is centered upon you!

God's biggest problem is not the big, important people. For one thing there are only a very few of them, really, and a surprising number of them are aware of their God-given opportunities just because they hold positions heavy with responsibility. No, ordinary one talent people are God's biggest problems because of the devilish notion that what we are and what we do is of very little moment except, perhaps, to a very small circle of relatives and friends. Whereas God has big plans, as God counts the word big, for us.

Do you begin to see why our Lord chose the one talent man and put him under the spotlight? And why he was so hard on him? Because that man is you. And God wants you to know, whether you believe it or not and no matter how incredible it may seem to you, that all heaven is at this very moment wondering about you and what kind of a person you are going to be; because the only kind of heaven God knows for this earth is the heaven he can bring to the earth only through you.

101

And it came to pass, that, as the people pressed upon him to hear the word of God, he stood by the lake of Gennesaret, and saw two ships standing by the lake: but the fishermen were gone out of them, and were washing their nets. And he entered into one of the ships, which was Simon's, and prayed him that he would thrust out a little from the land. And he sat down, and taught the people out of the ship. Now when he had left speaking, he said unto Simon, Launch out into the deep, and let down your nets for a draught. And Simon answering said unto him, Master, we have toiled all the night, and have taken nothing: nevertheless at thy word I will let down the net. And when they had this done, they inclosed a great multitude of fishes: and their net brake. And they beckoned unto their partners, which were in the other ship, that they should come and help them. And they came, and filled both the ships, so that they began to sink. When Simon Peter saw it, he fell down at Jesus' knees, saying, Depart from me; for I am a sinful man, O Lord. For he was astonished, and all that were with him, at the draught of the fishes which they had taken: and so was also James, and John, the sons of Zebedee, which were partners with Simon. And Jesus said unto Simon, Fear not; from henceforth thou shalt catch men. And when they had brought their ships to land, they forsook all, and followed him.

Luke 5:1-11

12.

+ + +

When the Lord Smiles on You

One of the most fascinating characters to walk the New Testament stage is the brash, fiery, and impetuous apostle, Peter. And not least among his fascinations is the light which his career throws upon the relation between what we call "good luck" or the "breaks" in life, and God's attitude toward individuals like you and me.

This is a thorny problem in a world like ours which, for all of its brave front, is far more superstitious than it cares to admit. It's a world which assumes that you have to get the "breaks" if you are going to get very far; a world which assumes that some people are born under a lucky star and others apparently are not; a world which assumes that good luck plays perhaps the dominant part in the ultimate outcome of our lives.

And for those of us who profess a faith in God this "good luck" seems to be tied up in some mysterious way with the eternal providence of God. If God smiles on you, you are led to conclude that there will be an upturn in your fortunes or luck; and if he doesn't, well, things are apt to get pretty grim, and make no mistake about it.

So let's take a look at a case history, the case of the "man called Peter," because his career began with a tremendous stroke of good fortune and ended, so tradition has it, on a cross. And, oddly enough, it was *all* tied up with the fact of God's smiling on him, not just the good fortune at the beginning of his career but the tragic end of it, too!

It began back there one ordinary day when, the night's work done, Peter was cleaning up his fishing gear on the beach and Jesus came by. At first Jesus asked if he could use Peter's boat as a pulpit. Later he told Peter to push off and try his fisherman's luck again. Peter thought it a silly idea, since his luck had been particularly poor that night, but he decided to give it a try anyway. And what happened, you remember, was a fisherman's dream come true: not just one boat loaded to the gunwales with fish, but two! So full, that both boats almost sank. It doesn't take a great deal of imagination to picture the next day's headlines in the Galilean Herald Tribune: "Local Fisherman Hits Jackpot."

Peter's great luck that morning has its counterpart all over the radio and TV map these days, only doubled and quadrupled, of course, since everything we do these days is bigger and better in every way, including our jackpots. Not too long ago I happened to watch a TV show where a woman won one of the largest of the TV jackpots and the announcer kept asking her over the phone, "Are you excited? Is your little boy awake yet? Have the neighbors started ringing your doorbell? They haven't? Well, they will." And they did, along with their congratulations and cries of, "What wonderful luck! You certainly deserved it! You must live right!", and all the other clichés appropriate to such occasions.

Now, by way of contrast, let us flash back to the general reaction to Peter's great good luck in hitting the jackpot on the lake of Galilee. There, kneeling down in the mess of fish, is Peter, awe written all over his face, crying, "Depart from me, for I am a sinful man, O Lord!" His companions are not slapping him on the back or congratulating him on his good fortune or telling him that he must have "lived right," because they, too, are struck dumb with awe.

That's the end of Act I of the little drama entitled, "When the Lord Smiles on You."

Act II follows immediately with a surprising turn of events. So far as we can discover, Peter never did cash in on his good fortune. No neighbors came to break down his doors and whoop it up until far into the night. No trip to Bermuda. No closets stuffed with new clothes. No diamond wrist watches. No maid service. And no $1,000 bonds to take care of the taxes. Just the quiet voice of Jesus of Nazareth: "Fear not, henceforth thou shalt catch men."

When the overloaded boats reached shore, Peter, James, and John left their boats, left the torrent of fish to the bewildered and excited crowd, left everything to go off on a new kind of adventure—following Jesus, a man they had known only a few hours.

So ends Act II. A considerable passage of time occurs between Act II and Act III.

Act III opens a number of years later with Peter, an old man now, bending over a letter he is writing to some of the men this big fisherman had "caught" through the years. The times were rough. The movement they had started years ago back there on the shore of Galilee had spread so far and so fast that the government was taking violent measures to stamp it out. Persecution, torture, and death lurked around every corner for those who would follow Jesus. Now the old fisherman wants to write and encourage them in the face of it. He is getting along toward the end of his letter: "Beloved, think it not strange concerning the fiery trial which is to try you, as though some strange thing happened unto you: but rejoice. . . . If ye be reproached for the name of Christ, happy are ye. . . . If any man suffer as a Christian . . . let him glorify God."

Not long after, the curtain falls with the salty old Peter crucified—head down, they say. He had followed Jesus—to the death. So ends the drama, "When the Lord Smiles on You."

This is certainly not the way we write such stories in life today. We are inclined to follow the theory developed in some places in the Old Testament that if the Lord smiles on you (and he will if you obey him), then good luck will follow you all the days of your life. A good life is supposed to get the "breaks"; an easy and prosperous life free from unusual trouble, hardship, or suffering.

Even those who ought to know better think of God in childish terms—those who have been exposed, at least, to the cross, which certainly indicates that the good life may very well find the going rough. The Lord, like little pussy in the nursery rhyme, will "love me because I am good." And if the Lord does love me, so this theory runs, and does send a bit of good luck my way once in a while then it's really no more than I deserve! Honestly, now! If you do have a stroke of good luck isn't the normal reaction, yours and mine, "Well, it's about time!" I have never yet run across anyone who did have a bit of good luck who wasn't eager to point out all the hard luck he'd had before and that it was about time the breaks began to come his way.

So now, let's wipe the slate clean of all these foggy and unchristian notions about luck and it's relation to God's attitude toward us. Let's take a good long look at Exhibit A in the New Testament as to what really does happen when the Lord smiles on you as he smiled on Peter out there in his fishing boat. To be sure, when the Lord smiles on you it may mean money in the pocket as it most certainly did for Peter in this instance. But the strange thing about that is that the money immediately meant nothing to Peter! Once he recognized that his good fortune was of God, he lost all interest in the fortune and could think only of God, of his own unworthiness in God's eyes, and of what God would have him do.

When God smiles on you, then, it may mean good fortune or good luck, as it did here for Peter in terms of wealth, and as it did for numbers of others in the New Testament in terms of health. But if you recognize this good fortune as coming at the hand of God, it will send you, too, to your knees with the cry, "Depart from me, for I am a sinful man, O Lord."

But when God smiles on you, it may also mean suffering. "But and if ye suffer . . .," Peter was writing and Peter remembered plenty of it in later years, ". . . happy are ye." The fact that God smiles on you doesn't necessarily bring good luck as we normally think of it; it brought a martyr's death to all but one of the twelve on whom he first smiled back there in Galilee. So, whatever it is that may be haunting you in your life now: illness or the threat of it, worry, or loneliness, or a marriage that isn't working out quite the way you'd hoped it would, a job that doesn't seem to be getting you very far, children that didn't turn out the way you'd planned, or whatever it is that we lump together under the label of bad luck, none of it is necessarily evidence that God has not and is not now smiling on you.

What, then, does it mean when the Lord smiles on you? Well, this much is certain. He has a job for you to do and he calls you to enter with him into the greatest adventure life has to offer: to create with him a new life and a new world.

In the light of that possibility Peter, James, and John forgot all about their good luck, their sudden wealth. They were intent on far more urgent business. Henceforth good luck and bad luck, as the world looks at them, would be meaningless apart from God's will and all he would have them do. If good luck came, well and good; if bad, "happy are ye." Happiness was no longer tied to the skirts of wealth or health or a stroke of good fortune. Happiness was to do the will of God come what may!

Happiness on these terms is not here today and gone tomorrow, dependent upon our moods or the moods of outward circumstance, dependent upon whether the sky is sunny or cloudy. It's the deep, steadying happiness of a man who knows that God *has* smiled on him.

That's why you find this happiness in the oddest places: a social worker knee-deep in dead-end kids; a housewife eking out a bare existence in a third-story cold-water flat;

a woman, hopelessly crippled, going about her daily chores as if her legs were perfectly sound; a man of eighty years cheerfully facing a major operation; a young girl giving up wealth, luxury, and comfort to marry a struggling, young teacher. Every here and there, in the odd corners of life, you will run across, as I have, these radiant souls who have found happiness not by looking for it and not riding on the tail of good luck, but simply by opening their eyes to see God's smile upon them, knowing that he has called them to do a job where they are.

That is what it really means when God smiles on you: not money in the bank, good health, or a trouble-free life, but rather the facing of the burden of these years with hope in your hearts and a song on your lips, knowing that you have become a part of God's creative and redemptive purpose in our world. Then, like Peter, you won't care very much whether your portion of luck is good or bad. You'll be much too busy!

The Lord was my stay. He brought me forth also into a large place.

Psalm 18:18b-19a

13.

+ + +

This Is the Life!

There are some words from the Eighteenth Psalm which always strike me as particularly appropriate for summertime. These words are a liturgical announcement, as it were, of the season when men shed their responsibilities and their formal clothes and head for the great open spaces. "The Lord was my stay. He brought me forth also into a large place." It's almost as if the Bible were bestowing its blessing here upon our summer excursions to the mountains, lakes, and seashore.

For the motive behind these excursions of ours is precisely this: to be "brought forth also into a large place," to free ourselves, if only for a few hours or days, from the restrictive and confining atmosphere of four walls, of streets, and buildings, and towns, and to achieve some measure of the expansiveness and roominess which the wanderer finds on a hilltop or at the edge of the sea.

And this is a true instinct, this desire we have to get out into the open. The human soul is meant for freedom and becomes restive and discontented if it is forever beset by restrictions and confinements. Thus when we take our bodies away from the physical confinements of city life out into the open, a voice within whispers authoritatively, "This is the life!" This, we know instinctively, is how life really ought to be lived, where there's room for a body to move around without forever tripping over curbstones and back fences and streetcar tracks, where the air blows fresh and sweet and a man has the urge and the opportunity to stretch and expand.

The difficulty, of course, is that this normal yen to get out of the hot city into the great open spaces is seasonal and temporary. It's only a respite, a fleeting experience of a day, a week, or a month. And for most of us the experience itself is confined and restricted by the fact that the end of it is always pressing hard on the beginning of it. But these seasonal flights into nature's open spaces at least give us an inkling as to what the psalmist is talking about.

Obviously he is not talking about summer excursions into God's great out-of-doors, but is drawing an analogy for the deeper truth. Just as the body exults in the freedom and roominess of nature's great open spaces, so does the soul of a man exult in the freedom and roominess which comes from faith in God.

This Eighteenth Psalm was written in just such an exultant mood, a triumphant song of one man's faith in God, "my rock, my fortress, my deliverer, my high tower . . . He brought me forth also into a large place." The immediate occasion for it was an ancient V-Day, a military victory. The poet is saying that the same sense of release and roominess which a nation experiences on V-Day is the sense of release and lift and spaciousness which God would have you enjoy every day.

Here, then, is a sure and certain touchstone for the faith we hold to determine whether it is really true to the genius of the Christian religion: If it does lead you out into life's great open spaces, if it does set your soul free from the cramping and constricting fears and evils of life. High religion, then, is not the restricting, confining, negative thing so many pseudo-religious people have made of it with their prim lips pursed in self-righteous disapproval of the full-blooded antics of the unsaved.

One of the most persistent heresies which has plagued the Christian church has been the notion that religion in general and Christianity in particular is restrictive and confining, and that it is narrow and inhospitable to new truth and fresh insights. The unfortunate result of this malignant and crippling heresy has been that many a red-blooded man with an active and inquiring mind has been seized by a severe attack of spiritual claustrophobia whenever he approaches a church or a gathering of church people. He fears the air will be stagnant, the ceiling low, and the walls will press him close on every side.

And, let's face it. His fears are not altogether groundless. Good sincere churchmen, both clergy and lay, have frequently pared down Christ's abundant life to a petty, puny kind of existence. They have taken the broad sympathies of Christ and narrowed them down to a provincial concern for respectability. They have taken his magnificent faith in the Father-God and compressed it into the sterile acceptance of orthodox catch phrases. They have taken his high morality and chopped it down to the petty, negative virtues of abstaining from certain varieties of indoor sports. It is an insidious and deadly heresy because it warps and twists the full, sweeping grandeur of the Christian faith and leaves it a stricken, deformed, and sickly shadow of the real thing.

Small wonder, therefore, that people are repelled rather than attracted by what they sometimes see parading around as evidence of what Christianity can do for you. Here, for example, is the daughter of a demanding mother, apparently motivated by life's highest good, unselfishness, or (putting it more positively) sacrificial love. Yet she is a living example of the perversion of that love. Urged on by a hard and narrow sense of duty, she has given herself completely to the demands of her widowed mother. She lives with her, supports her, is dominated by her until she has no longer any friends of her own, no life, no plans, no future she can really call her own. And all this in the name of unselfishness! The tragedy of it is that not only has the daughter's life been twisted and warped, but the mother's as well.

Or, in reverse, here is the unselfishness of a mother giving herself wholly to the welfare of her son, dominating him, making decisions for him, picking his friends, his school, his career—all, she would protest, in his best interests! But what is left is the deformed shell of a young man, his personality dwarfed and scarred almost beyond help. And this, too, in the name of sacrificial love!

Or here is a man whose religion is bounded north, south, east, and west by "thou shalt nots." He picks his way cautiously and successfully through life, avoiding all the scarlet as well as the petty sins. He doesn't commit adultery or swear, doesn't steal or play golf on Sunday, doesn't lie or tell dirty stories. And then, congratulating himself on avoiding these and other hazards, trips and falls flat on his face over the worst hazard of all—self-righteous pride.

No wonder, then, that many a man draws the mistaken conclusion that religion is a narrow, confining business which restricts rather than releases. And yet the root meaning of that old-fashioned word, salvation, is "to be wide" or "spacious." Salvation is a vast roominess under God. If anyone ever doubts the reality of sin in this life all he has to do is to look at what good religious folk have sometimes done to the meaning of this grand, spacious word: salvation!

For, from the very beginning of the Bible with the creation of a universe which has been expanding at breathless speed ever since, to the end of the Bible with its vision of a new heaven and a new earth where even the restriction of space is done away with, the theme of it all is room, spaciousness under God. The psalmist sings of it: "The Lord brought me forth into a large place." The prophets announce it: "As the heavens are higher than the earth, so are my ways higher than your ways. . . ." Paul is captivated by it: "That ye . . . may be able to comprehend . . . what is the breadth and length and depth and height." And at the very center of it all is our Lord: "I am come that ye might have life and have it abundantly."

How is it possible that we have made of this exultant spaciousness the dull, cramped business of placing one cautious and respectable foot in front of another and called it religion? Whatever else you may care to say about the Christian faith, it's not restricting, confining, tame, or dull. On the contrary—it sings. It opens up vistas for the mind. It offers release, spaciousness for the soul. I'm not saying there's no depth to it! The cross stands at the center of it. But it is the very depth of it—looking sin and death squarely in the face without flinching—which gives it its height and reach. Once a man grasps even a glimmer of what it offers, a voice within declares authoritatively, "This is the life! For this was I born."

But not only does this faith bring us into a "large place" where the soul has room to stretch and expand. It also breaks down the walls which divide us from each other, the confining and restricting prejudices which degrade and enslave whole groups of men because of their ancestry, their creed, or the pigment of their skins. For look at the fences men build, not only around their fields and homesteads, but around themselves. With the stones of prejudice and the brick of pride they fence around so neatly their little patches of mediocrity: "We are white! We are Protestant. My family traces its ancestry back. . . ." But something there is in life that keeps wanting to break these artificial barriers down.

In Robert Frost's poem, "Mending Wall," he tells of the annual spring chore when two neighbors walk along the stone wall which divides their properties, each on his own side, picking up the boulders which have toppled from place during the winter. The poem begins,

> Something there is that doesn't love a wall,
> That sends the frozen groundswell under it,
> And spills the upper boulders in the sun. . . .

The poem, of course, is a parable. Unless constantly and persistently rebuilt, these old, familiar stone walls lacing the New England countryside are gradually but inevitably leveled. "Something there is that doesn't love a wall."

Wherever in life men build up these artificial barriers, something there is that keeps everlastingly at it, quietly and persistently tearing them down.

There was a dramatic instance of it reported in the press a while ago when a car driven by a white man hit a car driven by a Negro. The Negro offered to exchange the customary credentials but the white man refused and became abusive.

The next scene took place in the police court where the judge found the white man guilty of disorderly conduct and gave him his choice of a ten-dollar fine or three days in jail. The white man, lacking the ten dollars, protested that he was a good family man and didn't belong in jail. Whereupon the Negro offered to pay his fine. The judge refused the money and gave the white man a suspended sentence.

In the last scene, the white man was going out the door, his arm around the Negro, repeating over and over, "You sure are a swell guy."

"Something there is that doesn't love a wall"—and you can write "Something" with a capital "S." It's God that doesn't love a wall.

But the walls we build are designed not only to keep the neighbors out; these walls are designed to keep God at his distance, too. For God is very pleasant to contemplate across the walls of selfishness and pride we build, and these barriers keep him from getting too familiar and intruding upon our private affairs; keep him from trampling on the well-cultivated gardens of our lives which are so concerned with me and mine, my interests, my family, my kind of people.

Good fences may make good neighbors when the neighbor's cattle are otherwise free to wander and trample the corn and the potato patch. But good fences never make good neighbors in the language of the New Testament where the cross rises up to dominate the landscape of man's relations with his neighbor and with God.

God never could abide the walls we build against each other and against him. He tried almost everything to tear them down. He sent the children of Israel into exile after exile. He held back a restraining hand when men tore at each other's throats across the walls they had built of race and nation. At length, not knowing what else to do, he stepped down into the midst of it all himself and they nailed him to a cross on a barren hilltop. It was all he could think of, his last and final gesture—tragic and victorious token of the groundswell of his love—which keeps tearing down the walls we build against each other and against him. He uses no coercion, no violence, just the gentle pressure of his love. "I died for you, my children."

Wherever you look within the faith we hold, there is this vast spaciousness under God who "brought me forth also into a large place." Here the soul of a man has room to stretch and expand and where between the souls of men the confining and restricting barriers they have built come slowly tumbling down.

The sure and certain touchstone of the Christian religion is this vast roominess under God. Once it gets hold of you, then, as during an excursion into nature's great out-of-doors, a voice within whispers authoritatively, "This is the life! For this was I born!"

PART IV

+ + +

"I saw the Lord . . . high and lifted up . . ."

Though I speak with the tongues of men and of angels, and have not charity, I am become as sounding brass, or a tinkling cymbal. And though I have the gift of prophecy, and understand all mysteries, and all knowledge; and though I have all faith, so that I could remove mountains, and have not charity, I am nothing. And though I bestow all my goods to feed the poor, and though I give my body to be burned, and have not charity, it profiteth me nothing.

Charity suffereth long, and is kind; charity envieth not; charity vaunteth not itself, is not puffed up, doth not behave itself unseemly, seeketh not her own, is not easily provoked, thinketh no evil; rejoiceth not in iniquity, but rejoiceth in the truth; beareth all things, believeth all things, hopeth all things, endureth all things.

Charity never faileth: but whether there be prophecies, they shall fail; whether there be tongues, they shall cease; whether there be knowledge, it shall vanish away. For we know in part, and we prophesy in part. But when that which is perfect is come, then that which is in part shall be done away. When I was a child, I spake as a child, I understood as a child, I thought as a child: but when I became a man, I put away childish things. For now we see through a glass, darkly; but then face to face: now I know in part; but then shall I know even as also I am known. And now abideth faith, hope, charity, these three; but the greatest of these is charity.

I Corinthians 13:1-13

14.

+ + +

Love Never Fails

Most preachers, including myself, are given at times—and not without cause—to bewailing the lack of religion in America today. Almost half the population has no church connection at all and of those who do far too many are something less than halfhearted about it. But that's not my concern at the moment. My concern runs in just the opposite direction to the widespread and growing interest in religion of all sorts and kinds in America today.

You don't have to look for evidence of it; it fairly shouts at you wherever you turn. On the magazine stands there is hardly an issue of any of the popular slick magazines which does not carry some article dealing with religion. On juke boxes syrupy and sentimental religious ballads vie with rock and roll. In the bookstalls religious books have been at or near the top of the best-seller lists for years now. In the movies Hollywood knows that a big, spectacular picture with a biblical background is almost sure-fire box office. And even a serious documentary film like *Martin Luther* amazed the motion picture industry with thousands of people lining up day after day in the larger cities across the country waiting to get in. The radio religious programs find hundreds of thousands of listeners, and on TV Bishop Sheen is a star of the first magnitude. Millions follow the adventures of the Fisher family on "This is the Life." Even the government feels the rising pulse of religious interest and inscribes its motto, "In God we trust," on its stamps as well as on its coins, and alters the pledge of allegiance to the flag to include the phrase, "one nation under God."

Naturally, the churches are taking advantage of all this interest in religion by embarking on the biggest church building program the world has ever seen, and cults and sects of all kinds are winning new converts every day. In the name of religion they offer everything from the salvation of souls, the healing of disease, and "peace of mind," to communication with the dead and the ability to handle poisonous snakes with impunity. America may not be in the center of a great religious revival but there certainly is a great lot of religious talk and activity going on.

Religion in America is free and you and I can thank God for it. A man can hold whatever faith he likes and give expression to it too. But this very freedom presents a problem. If religion is anything it is "of God." And how is a man to tell what in all this welter of religion in America is actually of God and what is not?

Paul faced this same question in a far more limited way back in Corinth in the first century. The church he had started there was growing fast and furiously. The people were expressing their religious convictions in all sorts and kinds of ways too. And the people at Corinth were perplexed. They could not tell which of all these religious expressions was most clearly "of God." So Paul sat himself down and gave them an answer in one of the most magnificent passages in the Bible, that grand thirteenth chapter of First Corinthians. Of all the expressions of religion, so he wrote, the only one that really counts in the end is love. Other expressions of religion may have value—preaching, teaching, healing, even the ecstatic "speaking with tongues." But unless they give expression to love they are quite worthless, because love alone "never fails."

Love, he says, is the indispensable mark of true religion. Faith? You can have faith enough to move mountains but without love it is nothing. Because faith without love ends in witch hunts and ugly religious wars and ridiculous absurdities like handling poisonous snakes. Charity? You can give away everything you own to feed the poor but unless the motive behind it is a deep concern for the well-being of others, it is trash. Self-sacrifice? You can give up your life and die a martyr's death and yet without love it is a wasted life; mock heroics, perhaps, or self-pity. Knowledge? You can know the Bible backward and forward; you can teach theology to scholars and yet without love it is worthless.

"Whether there be prophecies, they shall fail." Even the most inspired religious insight is not enough. "Whether there be tongues, they shall cease." Religious ecstasy is not enough. "Whether there be knowledge, it shall vanish away." Merely knowing a great deal about God is not enough. Only love . . . never fails.

What does Paul mean, "Love never fails"?

In the first place, it simply means that love outlasts anything else. You know the old saying, there is nothing permanent in this world except death and taxes. Well, Paul is saying that love is more permanent than death, taxes, or anything else you can think of. You know this well enough in your own experience. What is the one thing that holds your family together? Money? Health? A good reputation? A good job? Children? All of these can help, certainly. But every one of them can vanish overnight. Only love never fails. Even death cannot change it. You may know far better than I how the bond of love outlasts even the death of someone you love.

Or take it on a larger canvas. Here we are in a world anxious for some kind of permanent peace. So it fights its wars, writes its peace treaties, arranges its alliances, builds its stockpile of atomic weapons—all in the hope of finding a permanent peace. And all of this may be more than necessary. But a hundred years from now what of all that is going on in the world today will actually be permanent and lasting?

Paul Scherer tells [1] of how he went one day to look up the Crimean War with its Charge of the Light Brigade, its drums and guns, its death and suffering. He wanted to put against her proper background one lone woman, a lantern in her hand, going from bedside to bedside in the hospital barracks while soldiers kissed her shadow as she passed. He could remember her name, all right—it was Florence Nightingale; but he couldn't remember for the life of him what that war settled. Can you? What is permanent in this world? What is really lasting? Only love—which never fails.

And then, love never fails means that love always wins

[1] *The Place Where Thou Standest* (New York: Harper & Bros., 1942), pp. 151-2.

out in the end. That, I know, is hard to believe. So often love, kindness, mercy seem to end up in a dead-end street while suspicion, greed, hate, and violence take over. And yet if you think this is hard to believe, how much more difficult it is for people in other parts of the world. Here is Bishop Dibelius telling you what it's like in a congregation in the Russian sector of Berlin on a Sunday morning just a few years ago:

". . . a silent hopelessness lies over the congregation. All these people there beneath the pulpit have experienced the mercilessness of fate. For twenty years violence has ridden over their lives. Many have become doubtful about God, without quite being able to deny Him—else they would not be in church. And when one speaks to the younger generation about the love of God, the answer is a shrug of the shoulders. They point to the ruins that surround the church. They tell the story of their family: the father perished in a concentration camp; a brother was killed in battle; a sister was raped a score of times during the occupation of Berlin and in consequence is hopelessly diseased; the family dwelling was bombed to ruins. For five years they have not had a home fit for a human being; at work they are constantly spied on. The love of God? They have never known what that is." [2]

And yet out of that stark hopelessness these same people are stretching out their hands in trembling faith that despite everything love does win out in the end. And the only evidence they have for it is a cross. A cross: symbol of love's defeat. Men sneered at it, taunted it, spit in its face,

[2] Otto Dibelius, *The Christian Century*, LXVIII (January 31, 1951), p. 138.

and finally nailed it fast. And yet . . . a cross: triumphant symbol that you cannot defeat love.

Have you ever thought how utterly impossible it really is to defeat love? You can ignore it, or laugh at it, or get ugly and crucify it. But you cannot defeat it! "Father, forgive them for they know not what they do." You cannot defeat that! It keeps coming back, no matter what you do to it, to forgive you. And there is nothing you can do about it. Love never fails; it always wins out in the end.

That is why the New Testament keeps talking about love. That is why one-third of the Gospels are taken up with those last few days: the suffering, death, and resurrection of the Christ. It's not the miraculous cures of the sick that are central; not the prophecies and their fulfilment; not the Sermon on the Mount or the parables and teachings of Jesus. But the cross! That is central because it opens the door and lets a man look into the very heart of God to see there the love which never fails.

Are you sometimes bewildered by all this welter of religion in America? All the claims and promises which books and articles, churches, cults, and sects hold out to you? Are you tempted, perhaps, to think that God's greatest concern is to cure you or someone you love of a nagging illness? Or to give you some superficial kind of "peace of mind"? Do you wonder sometimes what God is really like, you hear men say so many and such confusing things about him? Here is the touchstone, the test for all of it. Don't take it from me. Take it from the whole of the New Testament. Ringing through every page of it: at the heart of the Gospels, at the center of Paul's epistles, the theme song of the writings of John, it is always the same—the love that is at the very heart of God laid perfectly bare and plain on a cross.

That cross speaks no uncertain word. It speaks to you in the kitchen with children underfoot; it speaks to you in the office surrounded by reports and filing cabinets; it speaks to you at your wits' end, not knowing how you are going to get through another week; or to you, perhaps, facing the latter part of life lonely and a little afraid. That cross casts its lengthening shadow across all the days and all the concerns of the days—the love that never fails. Do to it what you will: forget it, ignore it, shoulder it aside impatiently as sentimental and impractical—yet it keeps coming back like the return of spring, this amazing, undiscourageable, eternal, and triumphant love that is God.

If any religion in America today is truly of God, this love on a cross will not fail to be at the very heart and center of it.

And when they drew nigh unto Jerusalem, and were come to Bethphage, unto the mount of Olives, then sent Jesus two disciples, saying unto them, Go into the village over against you, and straightway ye shall find an ass tied, and a colt with her: loose them, and bring them unto me. And if any man say ought unto you, ye shall say, The Lord hath need of them; and straightway he shall send them. All this was done, that it might be fulfilled which was spoken by the prophet, saying, Tell ye the daughter of Sion, Behold, thy King cometh unto thee, meek, and sitting upon an ass, and a colt the foal of an ass. And the disciples went, and did as Jesus commanded them, and brought the ass, and the colt, and put on them their clothes, and they set him thereon. And a very great multitude spread their garments in the way; others cut down branches from the trees, and strawed them in the way. And the multitude that went before, and that followed, cried, saying, Hosanna to the Son of David: Blessed is he that cometh in the name of the Lord; Hosanna in the highest. And when he was come into Jerusalem, all the city was moved, saying, Who is this? And the multitude said, This is Jesus the prophet of Nazareth of Galilee.

Matthew 21:1-11

And when he was come near, he beheld the city, and wept over it, saying, If thou hadst known, even thou, at least in this thy day, the things which belong unto thy peace! But now they are hid from thine eyes. For the days shall come upon thee, that thine enemies shall cast a trench about thee, and compass thee round, and keep thee in on every side, and shall lay thee even with the ground, and thy children within thee; and they shall not leave in thee one stone upon another; because thou knewest not the time of thy visitation.

Luke 19:41-44

15.

+ + +

Ride on to Die

It was a queer kind of day, that far-off day in Judea, when Jesus entered the Holy City in triumph. It was a day of contrasts: of light and shadow, of climax and anticlimax, of frustration and fulfilment, of tears and hosannas!

Excitement was running high as it does on any great festive occasion and the natural excitement of the passover festival was heightened by this strange procession winding its way to the gates of the city. There at the head was a quiet figure of a man riding along while all about him crowds were gathering, curious at first, but soon they were shouting and singing and turning the place upside down for him. There was a moment when a strange hush fell over the crowd and those close by said that tears came to his eyes as he looked at the city. But the damper on their spirits lasted only for a moment. The shouts went up again, "Hosanna to the Son of David!"; the children sang again, "Blessed is he that cometh in the name of the Lord!" And everyone grabbed anything they could lay their hands on, branches from the trees, clothing from their backs, and threw it for a carpet in his path. Surely something amazing was about to happen!

Now watch how the story ends. For the point of it all is not what happened on that first Palm Sunday but what didn't happen! So—shouting and singing, laughing and nodding gaily to their neighbors, the crowd swept through the city gates and into the open place before the temple. There Jesus dismounted. The crowd, tense with anticipation, watched his every move now, stealing a glance at the heavens every once in a while for the sign that was sure to come. For was this not the Messiah? The chosen one of God who would bring legions of angels to establish the kingdom of Israel as God's kingdom forever and ever. . . . Today! Any moment! The crowd grew quiet. Only a low murmuring now as they watched him go into the temple. Their eyes glanced again at the heavens and back again to the door of the temple. Time passed. There was an uneasy restlessness. Nothing happened. Then slowly, one by one, the crowd melted away. And all that was left was an eerie silence and an empty feeling in their hearts.

No story ever built up to a greater anticlimax. It is quite obvious the writers of the Gospels could not get the flat taste of it out of their mouths. Listen how Mark ends his account of it: "He . . . went into the temple; and when he had looked around at everything, as it was already late, he went out to Bethany with the twelve." And that is the end of this story of the singing and shouting, the hosannas and the entry into Jerusalem in triumph!

Something quite obviously failed to come off here. It was a tremendous build-up for an equally tremendous let-down. It was indeed a queer kind of day. Just about as

queer as life! And the key to it, I think, is to be found back
there in that brief moment when Jesus, rounding a bend in
the road, saw the city nestled in its hills like a jewel in its
setting and broke down: "If thou hadst known, even thou,
at least in this thy day, the things which belong unto thy
peace! But now they are hid from thine eyes."

From that moment on the story is not the simple one of
a delirious crowd welcoming its hero as the promised
Messiah who would establish his reign in power. The story
takes on a double meaning and from that double meaning
arises its profound message for our world. Christ had taken
great care to prepare this entrance into the city so that his
meaning could not possibly be mistaken. He entered precisely as the prophets had said the Messiah would, right
down to the last detail. But he was a different Messiah from
the one they thought they were welcoming with palms and
hosannas. They thought he was riding on to set up his
reign as King of the Jews in triumph over the rest of the
world. He knew that he was riding on to die!

But the eternal appeal of the Palm Sunday story is not
merely its haunting ending, nor indeed that it is an intriguing
story with a double meaning. This is not history told in
the past tense at all. You and I are there! Not in the sense
of the TV program where we watch a fascinating re-enact-
ment of a dramatic incident in history. This story comes
alive in a different sense. Our whole world is there in that
story. Back there in the background is the indifference of
mighty, pagan Rome confident in its military power, intent
on its emperor worship and quite unaware that anything
significant at all was going on that spring day at the gates
of Jerusalem. And so today, mighty, pagan Russia broods

in the background, thinking its thoughts, planning its plans, intent on its emperor worship and quite oblivious to the palms and the hosannas of Christians.

And back there again in the more immediate background is the indifference of the well-to-do in Jerusalem that day, mildly amused or possibly annoyed by this peasant outburst over an up-country rabbi. And so today, in the more immediate background are the indifferent in our own country, amused or annoyed by the traffic jams caused by the Palm Sunday crowds going to and from the churches.

And then back there in the foreground is the enthusiasm and abandon of the multitude welcoming its Lord, blissfully unaware that the God they thought they were welcoming was a god of straw, a god fashioned by their own unreliable hands. And so today you and I are there, too, somewhere in that multitude singing hosannas but secretly wishing this were the climax, the end of it; that God would come and in one quick stroke establish peace among the nations with the American way of life the pattern for all of it; secretly wishing that he did not have to die! You and I are there in that multitude wishing desperately that somehow, some way, God would step in and suddenly solve the ugly and terrifying problems of our time: Russia and Red China, atomic power, and racial tensions, rather than have to pay the price of love and suffering.

I suppose that is why so many of us were unhappy with the outcome of the Korean war because we are impatient with halfway measures. We like a thing to be black or white and yearn for the easy, simple, and clear-cut solution. I suppose that is why, when eleven of our airmen were convicted as spies by Red China several years ago, the immediate reaction was to want to retaliate with an act of war, or a blockade, rather than to follow the more difficult but far wiser way of approaching the problem through the United Nations, so long as that way held out any hope for a settlement. If only the big problems of our world could be handled quickly and decisively without any loose ends dangling afterward! We used to think that if worst came to worst, we could always resort to war to solve our big problems and we even thought of war as perhaps God's answer to some very tough problems. For although the sacrifice and suffering would be intense for a time, at least there'd be an end to it and the problem would be solved. Now we know that no one wins a war any longer; we are all losers and the immediate problem at hand merely changes into a bigger and more complex problem. If only there were some quick, simple solution to the big and ugly problems of our world!

After all, what's the sense of a God who can't fix things up in a hurry if he's a mind to? That is why that shouting, singing crowd turned with a terrible consistency into a sullen, angry mob a few days later, crying "crucify" instead of "hosanna." That crowd wasn't fickle. It was frighteningly consistent! What is the sense in a God who lets the big and ugly problems in the world go unsolved?

Or does he? Do you remember not so many years ago when we were faced with a big, tough problem after the last war, the problem of several hundred thousand displaced persons in DP camps in Germany? To be sure, this was only one of a score of big problems left by the war, but it was one of the big ones. And I remember how it was when we broached the problem to the people of our churches.

The problem was too big, they said, too complicated for mere church people to handle. Besides, where would we find hundreds of thousands of jobs? And the housing? And think of the responsibility, to say nothing of the health of the economy, of bringing that many more people into a country already burdened by a number of unemployed. But soon in response to the appeal made in churches across the country, here was a family which said, "I'll take one." And then a church said, "We'll take two." And a business concern said, "We can take care of five." And before very long those refugees were coming over in a steady stream until that big, tough problem was solved. A mass migration of many thousands of people was made possible on the basis of one man here and another family there, willing to step out in faith that perhaps this is the way God solves the big and ugly problems of our time.

I suspect I know what you are thinking now. We are talking about the big and ugly problems of our world, Red China and the Communist threat, refugees, racial tensions, depressed and poverty-stricken areas scattered here and there all over the earth, each a possible spark for an atomic war. And I hark back to one relatively minor problem solved on the basis of individual response. Yet I submit to you that ultimately our world problems are just about that size. Granting, of course, that the solution for these big and ugly problems is hardly simple and requires the most astute statesmanship at high levels, yet in the final analysis they involve people, individual people, one by one, who are your immediate concern and mine.

I know how impractical that sounds to you. And yet that is exactly the kind of answer our Lord used to give to men when they asked him about the big problems of their world. "What must a man do to be saved?" they asked him. That is what we would like to know too! What must the world do to be saved from the mess it's in right now? And our Lord replied, "Keep the laws of God: Love the Lord thy God and thy neighbor as thyself." "Yes, yes," they replied impatiently, "we know all about that, but get to the point." So he went on, "A certain man traveling down from Jerusalem to Jericho fell among thieves . . ."

Very nice-sounding it was, too, that parable of the good Samaritan. The disciples and those who heard it were very much impressed. But all the time in the back of their minds, though they knew that like all decent people they must be kind to their neighbor in need, they knew that *that* simply could not be all there was to it. The eternal salvation of the world in a simple story of a kindly traveler? What about all those other people who did not love their neighbors, the Romans, for instance, or the Russians and Red China? Loving one's neighbor was good, sound policy, no doubt, and it was a pity more people did not do it more often. But even at best it was a long, slow, roundabout business. Surely God must have a more concrete and direct answer than that! The kingdom of God, they protested, God was going to establish that, wasn't he? And then these other people had better watch out. There was going to be swift and terrible judgment when God established his kingdom for good and all.

And then one morning these thoughts running in the back of their minds began to bubble and seethe because Jesus sent for an ass and a colt, the foal of an ass, and set out for the Holy City exactly the way the prophets said the Messiah would when he came to establish his kingdom. Before you knew it, they were pounding each other on the back and shouting hosanna and pulling branches from the trees and cloaks from their backs. The day had finally come! No more of this slow, roundabout business of painfully loving one neighbor after the other until kingdom come. Today he would give them God's big and dramatic answer to the big and ugly problems of their world. And the answer he gave them? A cross.

And it is still the way of it. You and I are in that crowd wishing desperately God would step in and provide an easy, simple, dramatic answer for our world. But he won't. He has too much respect for us. Way back at the beginning of things God took man into partnership and gave him dominion over all of this created world of ours. He will not go back on that. But he will and does show us the way of creative obedience and suffering. And if you and I respond in love and trust, and if, consequently, peace in our world begins to take root and grow, it will be because a man rode into Jerusalem one day, not to set himself upon a throne, but to enthrone his cross in the hearts of men like you and me.

And returning from the tomb they told all this to the eleven and to all the rest. Now it was Mary Magdalene and Joanna and Mary the mother of James and the other women with them who told this to the apostles; but these words seemed to them an idle tale, and they did not believe them.

Luke 24:9-11 (RSV)

16.

+ + +

No Idle Tale

Suppose you had been there with the disciples and the others grieving over the death of Jesus when a group of women burst in on you with a story of an empty tomb? How would you have reacted? Listen again to the end of Luke's account of the Resurrection: "And returning from the tomb, they told all this to the eleven and to all the rest. Now it was Mary Magdalene and Joanna and Mary, the mother of James, and the other women with them who told this to the apostles; but their words seemed to them an idle tale, and they did not believe them."

Well, what would you have said? Excitable women, no doubt, nerves overwrought, given to seeing things that aren't there, hearing voices no one else hears! Like so many women, making mountains out of molehills and molehills out of mountains, their story of the empty tomb sounded to the good, solid, feet-on-the-ground disciples—men, of course—like an "idle tale," a story for conversation over the teacups but hardly worth the consideration of sober men engaged in the serious business of grieving for a lost friend and leader. As we look back on it now, the distaff side may be heard to murmur complacently, "Just like men! So superior and cocksure in matters they think women know nothing about!"

And yet even the womenfolk need not deal too harshly with us, for to come back with a story of an empty tomb after you had watched the man suffer agonies and die before your eyes, taking all your hopes and dreams and faith with him, is hardly a story to be accepted on the bare face of it. Every known experience of ours is against it. If it wasn't a case of nerves getting the better of these good ladies, then it must have been a trick or sheer superstition. "But these words seemed to them an idle tale and they did not believe them." Can we really blame the disciples?

For the story of the Resurrection is still an idle tale for literally millions of people today. Not only for the worthy divine who preached one Easter morning on the noble theme, "Up-see-daisy," but also for many a man who wanders into church once a year on Easter—because? Because his wife and children put the pressure on him? Because he wants to be able to write home to mother that at least he went to church on Easter? Because it seems the thing most people do on Easter? But let that go. This striking phrase, an "idle tale," probes beneath the skins of some of us for whom Easter means far more.

There are some of us, you know, whose Christianity begins with Christmas and ends with Easter with nothing at all in between: No struggle in the wilderness, no curses or jeers, no bloody sweat, no dead and buried, no cross! It's not so far from the "Western Union theology" which one sharp columnist finds in the canned Easter messages foisted upon an apparently innocent public by that otherwise worthy company. One reads, "Here's hello from your Easter bunny. May your day be happy, bright, and sunny." And another, "Easter greetings across the miles. Here's wishing you a day of smiles." Apart from the sinister fact that each one extends beyond ten words, this columnist is right, of course. There is a theology there, the kind that looks upon Easter as being of the same stuff as the clinch at the end of the typical Hollywood product, the inevitable happy ending.

In the face of the grim aspect of our times, this shallow and optimistic caricature of Christianity is far more dangerous than one might suppose, for it provides the same kind of "escape" from the harsh realities of our world as the happy ending of a movie or a novel, but on a divine scale. Just think of Christmas and Easter; everything is going to turn out just dandy for everybody. Merry Christmas, Happy Easter and best wishes to everybody all around!

Certainly I don't want to darken the joy of Easter for you, even if I could, but it is a joy, an optimism, with depth to it! The Resurrection is after all a resurrection from the grave. The victory is a victory over sin and death. It is not just bright and cheerful on Easter; there is a majesty to it precisely because the man who rose from the grave did not escape anything—the sorrow, the defeat, the suffering, the hatred, the scorn, the thorns, the nails, and the spear. Take the cross out of Easter, as more of us do, I suspect, than would care to admit to it, and what is left *is* nothing but an idle tale, a legend, a nursery rhyme, a day with about as much depth to it as St. Valentine's Day.

But the story told by the excited women to the incredulous disciples was no idle tale. First one of these men, and then another, had the same amazing experience until all of them who had seen the man die and had watched the body laid away, who had witnessed the Roman seal set upon the stone at the door of the tomb—all of these disillusioned and sorrowing friends and followers experienced the dead man alive!

However you may explain it, it certainly did not mean any inevitable happy ending for those who found it to be true. I wish you and I could get hold of this and hang on to it! Because you have heard them and so have I, these friends of ours who say that our faith is nothing but wishful thinking, creating a god according to our own specifications on whom we can rely for comfort in time of trouble and for protection in time of danger, a kind of cosmic crutch for those who will not or cannot stand on their own two feet.

Let them tell that to Stephen dying of the stones they threw at him for his faith in the Resurrection! Let them tell that to Dietrich Bonhoeffer facing a Nazi firing squad just before the end of the war because he would not budge from his faith in the Resurrection! Let them tell that to the nameless Christians in labor camps in Siberia and Manchuria right now. A crutch for weaklings, no less!

Certainly, there was no inevitable happy ending for those eleven disciples on that first Easter. Instead of going to bed to dream of how nice it was that everything worked out all right in the end, it drove spurs into them, goaded them into action, gave them courage and power, and for all of them no happy ending, either, no escape but rather stonings, mobs, imprisonments, death—and yet with a song all the way through to the end!

Sometimes I think you and I are tempted to observe the Resurrection of our Lord on Easter in much the same mood as a couple on their honeymoon might observe Niagara Falls at night. With all the beauty of the lights turning the mist into the colors of the rainbow, with the majestic roar of the water, it is one of the most stirring sights of our world. And yet that couple may be all unaware, perhaps, of the tremendous power latent in those tons of water crashing onto the rocks below to form the lovely mist—only a fraction of it harnessed to produce electric power. Meanwhile the couple watching it dreams of a cottage small by a smaller waterfall.

So with the Easter celebration. There is the loveliness and fragrance of the flowers, the majestic beauty of the Easter hymns and anthems, the glory of the ancient liturgy, and yet, perhaps, only a fraction of its latent power actually harnessed to life. And the Resurrection *is* an idle tale unless its power is harnessed and released in life.

It's just possible, of course, that we are afraid of it, afraid of what it might do to us if we gave it its head. A story appeared in one of the fiction magazines not long ago telling of four victims of the war in a veterans' hospital and of what happened when a miracle occurred one night and they walked right out of their wheel chairs and hospital beds and back into the normal activities of life in America again. One of them had resolved, as a result of the miracle, to lose no opportunity to read the Sermon on the Mount to any and all who would listen. The press, meanwhile, had splashed the story of the miracle across the country and crowds of the curious came to see for themselves and remained to listen, fascinated by the Sermon on the Mount on the lips of this ex-GI. Strangely enough, more than a few took it to heart. In a matter of days the whole country began to be turned upside down. The people poured out of the department stores and crowded into the churches. Businessmen began to get jumpy. The stock market slumped as this veteran went about saying, "Store not up for yourselves treasures upon earth. . . ." The whole country rocked on its foundations. Congressmen solemnly intoned that it was "un-American," and immediately initiated a full congressional investigation. Sober statesmen cornered the youth and begged him to take it easy, that the future of the country, of the world, was at stake. But he kept on reading and the people kept flocking to see and to listen. And how does the story end? Just as you might expect. False witnesses were found to say that the whole thing was a hoax. The frenzy began to die away. Finally one man, crazed by the loss of his money, shot him.

This is the Easter story in reverse. Here in Palestine was a man who lived the Sermon on the Mount first. Then, after the authorities thought they had shut him up for good, came the miracle, the Resurrection. But the explosive implications for our world are exactly the same, with this one rather important difference: The Easter story is not fiction. It is fact. A frightening fact, for it means that all that Jesus said, all that he did is eternally true! And once you give that its head it does turn our world upside down.

Is that it? Are we afraid of the explosive power of Easter and what it might do to us if we allowed ourselves to dream dreams for ourselves as large and vast as those of Jesus of Nazareth? No doubt it's safer to keep the Resurrection an idle tale; sniff the lilies, say a prayer or two, give voice to a well-modulated alleluia and let it go at that; go home with our lives undisturbed by the frightening fact of it.

Arthur Gossip draws this significant contrast between Anatole France and Jesus of Nazareth. Anatole France took a final look around toward the end of his life and gave it as his considered verdict that there is at least one thing of which we can be absolutely sure; that men are always smaller than they seem. Not at all, says Christ, not smaller, always bigger than they seem, bigger than they want to be.

If the Resurrection has anything at all to say to you, it is this: It paints a far grander picture of you than you could ever imagine or that possibly you might ever wish for yourself. You don't have to accept it. You can hide from it. Not even God will make you bigger or greater than you want to be. But at least it's no idle tale. It is a story with power for the brave, for you if you have the courage with Peter and Paul and the others to have your fling at life not as a little man with cautious little plans and cozy little dreams, but as a man with plans and dreams so big they cannot possibly end in bewilderment, defeat, or even death. Those are the plans and dreams God has for you on Easter. And it's no idle tale. It's all true.

For this cause I bow my knees unto the Father of our Lord Jesus Christ, of whom the whole family in heaven and earth is named, that he would grant you, according to the riches of his glory, to be strengthened with might by his Spirit in the inner man; that Christ may dwell in your hearts by faith; that ye, being rooted and grounded in love, may be able to comprehend with all saints what is the breadth, and length, and depth, and height; and to know the love of Christ, which passeth knowledge, that ye might be filled with all the fulness of God. Now unto him that is able to do exceeding abundantly above all that we ask or think, according to the power that worketh in us, unto him be glory in the church by Christ Jesus throughout all ages, world without end. Amen.

Ephesians 3:14-21

And Jesus called a little child unto him, and set him in the midst of them, and said, Verily I say unto you, Except ye be converted, and become as little children, ye shall not enter into the kingdom of heaven.

Matthew 18:2-3

17.

+ + +

The Extravagant Kindness

The trouble with Christianity is that it is always turning perfectly good, respectable virtues into hazards and stumbling blocks. Look, for example, at what it does to our very proper regard for prudence and caution.

Few virtues are more highly prized in our world. Who is the wise man in our day? He is the man who looks before he leaps, who has a sound insurance program, who wants a stable, reliable young man for his son-in-law, who plans a year ahead and joins Christmas and vacation clubs, who has a periodic physical examination and has his teeth checked twice a year, who carefully examines references and experience before hiring, who consults consumers' research before buying, and who plugs for a guaranteed annual wage and social security. Wisdom in our time has become almost equivalent to prudence and caution.

And certainly no one will deny the virtue in all this. The only trouble with it is that it makes it so very difficult for us to understand God! Because if prudence is a prime virtue in our world, extravagance is the word for God. Some men I know turn purple when they start to think of the government's extravagance in recent years. And yet compared with God's extravagance, the government is old Mr. Scrooge himself.

Just consider God's extravagance for a moment. To a prudent American businessman, carefully weighing supply and demand, market fluctuations, and the political and international climate a year or two hence before placing a big order, the way God runs the universe is simply inexplicable. Here is this universe expanding at unbelievable speed ever since the beginning of time. Infinite expansion for no observable purpose except, perhaps, to make us feel a little smaller than we already feel. Or here in all this vastness, which no man can possibly measure, is this infinitesimal earth of ours with most of nature's lush extravagance wasted on the tropics where no civilized person can stand for long the heat or the bugs. It doesn't make sense. Not to a prudent, orderly mind, at any rate.

Allan Watts compares the extravagance of nature with music at its highest: "The preludes and fugues of Bach, he writes, "are simply a complex arrangement of glorious sounds. . . . They need no programme notes to explain a moral or sociological message. . . . The intricate melodies flow on and on, and there never seems any necessity for them to stop. He composed them in tremendous quantities, with the same Godlike extravagance to be found in the unnecessary vastness of nature." [1]

But beyond sheer size and numbers is God's extravagance with beauty. Listen to Robinson Jeffers:

[1] *Behold the Spirit* (New York: Pantheon Books, Inc., 1947), p. 179.

Is it not by his high superfluousness we know
Our God? For to equal a need
Is natural, animal, mineral: but to fling
Rainbows over the rain
And beauty above the moon, and secret rainbows
On the domes of deep sea-shells,
And make the necessary embrace of breeding
Beautiful also as fire,
Not even the weeds to multiply without blossom
Nor the birds without music. . . .
The extravagant kindness. . . .[2]

Have you ever thought of God's love as extravagant? It is, you know. Suppose, for a moment, you had created a fine new world and peopled it with splendid little creatures made in your own image, written into their hearts a longing to know the God who had made them, given them the law of right and wrong, and granted them the freedom to choose. And then you had found that these marvelous little creatures were soon at each other's throats, hoarding or wasting the bounties of nature as the mood struck them, each one scrambling to get on top of the next. I wonder if you would not have lost patience and simply let them scramble. But God loved them.

So God did more. He whispered into the hearts of a few of the more sensitive among them, recalling the God who had made them, and the purpose for which they were made. Some few listened but more ignored or cursed these prophets, as they were called, and told them to mind their own business. You would probably have given up then.

But God did more. For at length God said to himself, "I shall go down and live among them, share their life, its

[2] "The Excesses of God," from *Be Angry at the Sun* (New York: Random House, 1941).

149

difficulties and struggles, even its death if need be. Surely if they can see and touch me they will listen to me and live in peace and joy with each other." So God stepped down. These little creatures listened for a while but soon they grew ugly, bared their teeth, and killed him. Surely if you or I had been God, that would have been more than enough.

But God did more! For God said, "I will show myself alive to them now so that nevermore will death hold any terrors for them; nevermore will they be left in ignorance or confusion about me or my love for them." So God did more and Christ rose from the dead. And I wonder if you or I would have bothered!

Surely if God had been prudent and cautious, measuring the probabilities of the return on his investment of love, he wouldn't have bothered either. But he did. That's the wonder of it—the extravagance of his love which gives itself without stint and asks nothing in return. And anyone who tries to describe it can only resort to extravagant language too. Listen to Paul, carried away by the extravagant kindness of God, every phrase brimming over and indicating more beyond: "riches of glory . . . length, breadth, depth and height . . . love surpassing knowledge . . . filled with all the fulness of God . . . exceeding abundantly above all that we ask or think. . . ." You just can't measure love like that. You can't be prudent and cautious and even come close to understanding what it's all about.

That is why our Lord was always drawn to those who had a reckless streak in them somewhere: a poor widow throwing her all into an offering bowl, surely an imprudent and foolish thing to do; a little man who climbed a tree like a curious child to get a look at him; disciples sufficiently short on caution and discretion to chuck their careers for a vision. Doubtless if Christ had chosen more prudent men he never would have found a Judas among them. But neither would he have found a Peter, a James, or a John!

And then there was that rich young ruler. He never quite made it. But when he forgot his dignity long enough to come running and fall in the road at his feet, our Lord loved him for it. You see, Christ had to find men who were willing to throw caution to the winds and forget the prudent counsels of the discreet if they were ever to catch a vision of this God who is so extravagantly kind.

If you wonder sometimes why this joyous note of extravagance and abandon is so foreign to us, so ill at ease in our ponderous theological discussions, so absent in our preaching, and so rare in our worship, the primary difficulty lies here: We take ourselves so seriously that we cannot conceive of a God who is not as serious-minded and cautiously ponderous as we are. Our sin, if you like, lies precisely at the point where we refuse to become the children of God because it is beneath our dignity. Religion is a serious business, of course! Only we take ourselves more seriously than we take God and his extravagant love. There's that pious solemnity, so often the mark of the clergy like myself, and never so apparent as in the ecclesiastical procession which almost borders on the ridiculous because one can never be quite sure whether we're taking God seriously or taking ourselves seriously taking God seriously!

I think that's why the story of the juggler going through

his act before the statue of the Virgin has such universal appeal. For here at least is a touch of reality—the natural exhibition of a man's best offered without self-consciousness or discretion to his God in the elemental forms of joyful expression.

And so it is that Christ takes a little child, puts him into the center of a circle of ponderous grownups and declares, "Except ye become as little children ye shall not enter the kingdom of heaven." Our Lord had a knack of putting the most profound truths into deceptively simple terms: "Except ye become as little children." So simple an analogy and yet bristling with suggestions, not least the child's delightfully unself-conscious joy in living. You and I smile tolerantly at the extravagances of childhood. And yet I suppose we will never know what God has in store for us until we do become as little children, get down on the floor on our hands and knees and *look up*, to see ourselves and life and death from that refreshingly divine perspective.

Look, for example, at what happens to those horizons Paul talks about, the length, breadth, depth, and height. From the viewpoint of a child, life's horizons are unlimited. The length of life is indeterminate. A year, so short for an adult, is a lifetime for a child, and death is but a door into another life which God out of his extravagance has provided. So with the breadth of life. No limits there, either. For the child, untouched by adult prejudice, there are no boundaries. White skin, black, or brown, what difference does it make other than just another instance of life's infinite variety and capacity for surprise? The horizon of depth may be an exception. And yet, even though as fleeting as a thundershower, who can fathom the exquisite grief of a child? And the dimension of height is equally limitless. Nothing is impossible. God is quite literally omnipotent, able to do exceeding abundantly beyond all that anyone can ask or think.

But let the child grow into an adult and watch the horizons close in, sometimes with terrifying effect. How readily, as life goes on, the limitless becomes limited. In no time at all the child who just yesterday risked life and limb to climb higher than anyone in the nearest tree, who laughed at the threat of catching cold in the rain, has learned to keep his feet on the ground and rubbers on his feet. For life's length is not so unlimited any more. Death comes nearer now, a door which closes on this life rather than opening on another.

The breadth of life contracts too. There are differences in people, it begins to appear, which go beyond the color of the skin. Only some folk make proper playmates, he learns, while others are all right for business transactions, and still others should more properly shine your shoes or run your elevators. As he moves into old age he suddenly wakes up one morning to find the breadth of life exceedingly narrow indeed, with his friends dying off, his family scattered to the winds, and the walls of loneliness closing in.

He finds, too, that the dimension of depth has been a delusion. Sin is for pessimists and gloomy theologians. He has learned that man is basically good and given a little more education, and some adjustments in plumbing and play-grounds, the kingdom of God will arrive day after tomorrow provided an H-bomb doesn't fall on him first.

As for life's height, Junior soon learns from his elders that stars are for dreamers and the sky for loafers. A good eight-foot ceiling keeps off the rain and is easily repaired with the help of a low stepladder.

So do the horizons move in for the cautious, prudent, careful man until his cozy little world threatens to suffocate him. One of the more horrible among horror stories pictures a man standing in a room with four walls, floor and ceiling all gradually moving in on him from every side. And there is no escape.

Now listen to Paul again: "That Christ may dwell in your hearts by faith . . . rooted and grounded in love, able to comprehend the breadth, length, depth and height . . . filled with all the fulness of God . . . able to do exceeding abundantly above all that we ask or think. . . ." It doesn't make sense! Except you become as a little child! Then this extravagant love of God begins to stir around in you until it surges through every thought, dream, and ambition. And suddenly the whole process of life's horizons steadily moving in on us goes into reverse! And the horizons move out in every direction.

The root meaning of that old word, salvation, as has been pointed out over and over again, means *room*—room for a soul to move around in. This is what Christ offers you—*if* you will toss aside your cautious prudence for a moment, get down on the floor on your hands and knees and look up at life through the eyes of a child. Then you will be "born again," as the Bible has it, and see life's infinite capacity for wonder and surprise—and the extravagant kindness which is at the heart of God!

Type used in this book: Body, 10 on 13 Janson; Display, Radiant
Paper: "RRR" Standard White Antique